T0013158

THE
MILLION DOLLAR
GREETING

THE MILLION DOLLAR GREETING

TODAY'S BEST PRACTICES FOR PROFIT, CUSTOMER RETENTION, AND A HAPPY WORKPLACE

DAN SACHS
WITH JANET SCOTT

APOLLO
PUBLISHERS

The Million Dollar Greeting: Today's Best Practices for Profit,
Customer Retention, and a Happy Workplace

Copyright © 2023 by Dan Sachs and Janet Scott.

All rights reserved. No part of this book may be used or reproduced in any
manner whatsoever without the written permission of the publisher, except
in the case of brief excerpts in critical reviews or articles. All inquiries should
be sent by e-mail to Apollo Publishers at info@apollopublishers.com.

Apollo Publishers books may be purchased for educational, business,
or sales promotional use. Special editions may be made available upon request.
For details, contact Apollo Publishers at info@apollopublishers.com.

Visit our website at www.apollopublishers.com.

Library of Congress Cataloging-in-Publication Data is available on file.

Cover design by Rain Saukas.

Print ISBN: 978-1-95464-180-8
Ebook ISBN: 978-1-948062-15-2

Printed in the United States of America.
First printed in hardcover in 2018.

CONTENTS

BY ALWYN SCOTT

A few years ago, my wife and I were shopping for ski gloves at the flagship store of an outdoor goods retailer, a Seattle company known for deep expertise and legendary customer service. We picked two pairs of gloves and asked a salesman which would be warmer.

"Impossible to say!" he replied, delightedly. There were simply too many variables, he said—would my wife use them in wet or dry weather, high or low altitude, snow or rain conditions?—to render a meaningful opinion. And he walked off.

We found this hilarious. Like Jack Black's comedic record-store salesman in the movie *High Fidelity*, this guy was so steeped in knowledge that he could not answer a simple question. Still holding the two pairs of gloves, we asked another salesperson, an older woman.

"This pair," she said without hesitation, and pointed to one.

We have told the story many times, and we gradually moved our business to another Seattle outdoor goods store that took itself a little less seriously. One that could tell us, straight off, which item was warmer.

Here, in a nutshell, is what *The Million Dollar Greeting* reveals: Why companies that sweat the details still fall flat with customer service—and how you can not only avoid those mistakes, but build a culture where they just don't happen.

It might seem simple. After all, customer service is as old as business itself. But the world is changing. We live increasingly in a disconnected, digital world filled with millennial customers and employees who see things quite differently than their parents did.

At Brooklyn Brewery, for example, founder Steve Hindy realized years ago that he needed to teach his customers about the history and many styles of beers if he hoped to sell the flavorful suds he was brewing. He started a "beer school" so employees could speak knowledgeably to customers.

More than thirty years later, the school is just as vital, in part because it appeals to new millennial workers, who tend to value a sense of authenticity far more than loyalty to a company.

That's why this book is timely. Through extensive on-the-ground research, *The Million Dollar Greeting* distills a unique formula that helps businesses of all sizes achieve consistently good customer service for millennials and older generations. That formula, combined with a wealth of practical examples, gives this book its extraordinary insight and value.

This isn't just feel-good stuff. It is a road map to much higher profits for leaders who use the formula correctly. Why? As we found with the ski gloves, good service brings loyalty and the willingness to pay more.

Would you be interested to know how global businesses such as the Amazon-owned shoe seller Zappos and the Hyatt Hotels chain use the formula to deliver the customer service that sets them apart?

Would you like to learn how Union Square Hospitality Group, which runs seventeen New York City restaurants, bars, and cafés, ensures top-notch experiences for customers, whether they are having antipasti at a rustic Italian bistro, southern barbecue at a jazz club, or Michelin-starred cuisine at the Museum of Modern Art?

What about smaller businesses? Ann Arbor food merchant Zingerman's and Chicago's Nick's Pub & Pizza put the principles to work on an intimate scale, achieving a bond with customers that keeps them coming back—and telling their friends.

I have known Dan since the 1980s, shortly after he graduated from Harvard, and have watched as he opened two highly successful restaurants in Chicago: Spruce and Bin 36. I marveled at the attention to detail and the relaxed, sophisticated atmosphere he and his staff created.

Not every company creates this kind of experience. I should know. I have seen all kinds of businesses in nearly three decades covering financial news as a reporter and editor at *Dow Jones*, *Wall Street Journal*, *Seattle Times*, *American City Business Journals*, and *Reuters*, a global news agency that reaches a billion people. Some companies know how to connect. Others simply don't get it.

Through extensive interviews with nine business leaders, Dan unearths the roots of their philosophies and reveals how they put them into practice every day.

Dan's candid hindsight about how he might have run his own restaurants better leads him to ask the questions you want answered and to pull together the insights into a coherent whole. The sections lay out the principles and themes in a clear, easy-to-digest way, and memorable anecdotes are throughout.

The world is changing. But giving customers a good experience is still the route to loyalty, a good brand, and profitable sales. Here is how businesses large and small deliver it. And how you can, too.

A BRIEF (BUT NECESSARY) HISTORY OF CUSTOMER SERVICE

I started thinking about this book a couple of years ago. After examining my own experiences as an independent entrepreneur, teaching at DePaul University in Chicago, and years of consulting, I began to see clear patterns emerge between leadership behavior and organizations that provide great customer service. I recognized that some organizations seemed to expend a lot of energy and focus in order to offer exceptional customer service, while others did not. This isn't a revolutionary observation, but I decided to dig a little deeper to find out what makes those "best in class" organizations tick. I dug so deep, in fact, that I wound up with this book, which showcases nine "best in class" companies and outlines the core principles their leaders have adopted to encourage and nurture great service.

I have spent most of my life working in the hospitality sector, and my career has taken me across the country. I began as a line cook and restaurant manager in New York City and eventually owned several restaurants in Chicago. I have known, worked with, or worked for some of the most respected leaders in the culinary industry. Perhaps more importantly, I grew up in an entrepreneurial home where taking care of your customer was emphasized from an early age. In many ways, I learned about customer service the "old school" way—by watching my father.

Of course, great customer service can be defined in many ways. From my perspective, it involves three key stakeholders: employees, customers, and shareholders. These are not unique components in any service company, but as our workforce begins to transition and more millennials assume positions of responsibility, organizational leadership is at an inflection point. The leaders profiled in this book realize this, and it's no coincidence that they focus so strongly on employees when talking about their vision for excellence. For this new generation, the old top-down management structure no longer provides the workplace satisfaction that it might have in years past. As a result, new leaders are changing the workplace dynamic in an effort to capture the hearts and minds of their employees and, ultimately, their customers.

And, as you will see, the employees of these organizations are not only engaged but also stimulated by their work. This synergy between a new management structure and employee engagement leads to remarkable results: consistently profitable companies with reputations for exceptional customer service and a cohort of employees who rank their organizations in the top tier of places to work in North America. The leaders profiled in this book exhibit clear patterns of belief, behavior, and purpose. Some are "Evangelists"—true believers who have organized their companies down to the smallest detail in an effort to ensure that each aspect of operations offers employees and guests alike a consistent experience. Others are "Transformers"—leaders who recognize that the workplace is changing and that their organizations need to meet the future head-on, with eyes wide open. Last, but not least, there are "Pragmatists"—leaders who recognize and embrace changes in the employee population and the workplace culture in order to deliver quality to their customers. Regardless of their paths, these leaders share a consistent message, which is that certain core values must be present for outstanding customer service to be delivered. These values are accountability, authenticity, culture, community, and vision.

Creating an organization that champions customer service not just in words but in deeds is hard work—there's no app for that. Yet, the leaders in this book have all developed systems to ensure that customers are not only treated well but, equally if not more importantly, employees are too—many even better than the customers.

Whether they consciously know it or not, many of the tools these leaders employ incorporate well-established tactics, some of which have existed for centuries as part of the hospitality sector of the service economy. Only as the workplace has slowly transformed in the past twenty to thirty years, have we started see these hospitality traits manifest themselves more commonly in other industries. Leaders in every industry who have embraced these tools have created organizations that differentiate themselves from the pack.

Of course, we all know there are no "perfect" leaders or companies. The strategies used by the leaders in this book will not apply to every company, and you may relate to some of the anecdotes more than others. Still, despite any shortcomings, this book illustrates how to move forward on a path that embraces a new generation of employees looking for meaning, authenticity, and a sense of community within the workplace. For these employees and their leaders, dedication to outstanding customer service may not be a religion, but it certainly could be a substitute for it.

IT ALL STARTS WITH HOSPITALITY, BABY

NO ONE SAID IT WAS GOING TO BE EASY

Consider this: over 80 percent of the United States workforce is part of the service economy (United States Department of Labor, Bureau of Labor Statistics, Employment by Major Industry Sector, 2016, most current available data).

Yet, most businesses spend only marginal time and resources to help frontline employees understand and appreciate the value of excellent customer service. While an organization may have clearly defined customer service training plans, we've all experienced enough varying levels of "service" to know that excellence is not easily taught or achieved. Moreover, despite overwhelming evidence of the economic value of high-quality customer service, according to the 2017 NICE in Contact CX Transformation Benchmark Study, there is an 18 percent gap between company and customer perceptions of service quality.[1] And given that happy customers are loyal customers, this raises an important question: Can a company afford the gap between customer perception and the quality of its service?

I believe the answer to that question is a fairly straightforward no. However, providing consistent service excellence is *hard*. Really hard, in fact. It's not that companies don't want to offer good service. But without a dedicated, consistent organizational approach, it's not going to happen. We've all experienced poor service from organizations within the hospitality sector—the very industry where good service is the very product that is being purchased. So how much can we really expect from an accountant or a telecom company? Add to the mix the fact that the new, younger workforce is unlikely to intuitively understand how to execute hospitality excellence, and you have a recipe for disaster.

According to the 2017 American Express Customer Service Barometer, more than seven out of ten respondents claim they spend more money with a company that delivers great service—and you, like me, may very well be one of these seven. Similarly, nine out of ten people claim that they would pay more to ensure superior service (Customer Experience Impact Report, Harris Interactive, 2010). The data shows that there is a direct link between an investment in hospitality training and profitability. So, what's the problem?

---

1   https://www.niceincontact.com/call-center-resource-finder/2017-incontact-cx-transformation-benchmark-study-business-wave.

To start, we need to understand the word *hospitality* and why its meaning extends far beyond your meal at a local restaurant or a hotel stay. There is an equation that describes the relationship between service quality and customer satisfaction:

$$\textsc{Hospitality} = \textsc{Empathy} + \textsc{Action}$$

Now, substitute the word "hospitality" for "service quality" and you can start to see the point. I spoke with Susan Salgado, founder and CEO of Hospitality Quotient, a New York-based hospitality consulting firm, and she explains hospitality this way: "Hospitality is about being on the other person's side. So, by our definition, in order to provide great service to any group of people, we need to put ourselves in their shoes and figure out what they want and deliver on that kind of experience." Communicating with empathy, however, can be tricky, especially for younger generations who have grown up communicating via text, Snapchat, and Facebook. Many of them haven't had as much personal human interaction as earlier generations, so it can be difficult for them to imagine walking in a customer's shoes. "In terms of millennials and what they're looking for—it's a low-touch, high-tech kind of interaction," says Salgado.

Moreover, even when people are trained how to empathize, they need to know how to take the information they glean and convert it into *action*. As Salgado explains, "What does your demographic want? What does your individual customer want? You need to tailor that experience to match that desire." If we accept that these are the right questions to ask about hospitality, then we can start to evaluate the tools that achieve hospitality success—primarily through understanding how leaders create an environment that fosters empathy with employees and, ultimately, customers. Mastering this equation can lead to a multitude of successes, both emotional and financial.

STARTING FRESH

Have you ever thought about how many times you encounter service in your daily routine? I have, and what I've come to realize is that I provide or experience a "service" (the idea of helping or doing work for somebody else) multiple times throughout the day, starting as soon as my alarm clock goes off. Because my interactions with others—family, friends, coworkers, and strangers alike—dominate my day, they also set the tone for my own behavior, which then influences my attitude toward others. This idea is nothing new, but it's very easy to lose track of how significantly our own actions can affect the people around us and vice versa.

Usually, my morning begins by waking my kids up and getting them ready for school, along with letting out and feeding our black poodle, who is the most compliant of all of them. It feels like a pretty mundane routine, day in and day out, and I'm sure many of you experience the same type of feeling, like you're on autopilot. But if I take a step back and think about it, my morning "routine" is actually the beginning of my own personal quality service delivery experience. And that delivery experience definitely varies, because if I'm honest with myself, I'm not a vessel of boundless energy and optimism every morning, though I wish I were.

Even if I manage to get the kids to school on time and myself to work without too much drama, we've still influenced each other. Having repeated this harried thirty-minute daily exercise thousands of times, I've learned a lot from it. Take the following situation, which happens more often than I would like it to.

> *It's a Tuesday. I'm out of bed a few minutes late and because I didn't plan for any extra time, I'm already behind my schedule of waking, feeding, and getting my kids ready for school. So, I rush them out of bed, let the dog out, find some food in the fridge, and start to get*

everyone moving. In the midst of preparing breakfast for the kids and the dog, there is little or no effort to interact. They're still tired and I'm rushed, so we don't greet each other with a smile or even speak. In fact, in the rush of the routine, I'm the only one who's normally saying anything at all, and usually I'm only reminding them to hurry up so I can get them to school on time. If we're lucky, we all get in the car in one piece and start rolling through stop signs on the way to school. If, God forbid, somebody forgets something (as is often the case), a dark cloud moves over the car, we turn around, and rarely speak for the rest of the trip.

You may argue that providing a meaningful experience for my kids early in the morning every single day is beyond a reasonable expectation. That's a lot of breakfasts to enrich! However, I have come to appreciate that the morning "rush" to get out of the house is a useful window into the concept of customer service generally. When thinking clearly, I know I should be treating my kids the way I want to be treated when I am picking up my coffee at the local deli or working with my clients throughout the day. It's easy to make excuses for not creating a memorable experience day in and day out, but in the end, creating a quality experience is what can make or break your day.

We've all read about, and can appreciate, the value of starting the day with a smile and a positive attitude. I'm not suggesting that life is a bowl of unicorns and strawberries, but smiling at the start of the day really does seem to take the edge off. Those days that I do slow down, I notice how much more positive my interaction with my kids is. All of us feel less stressed and more relaxed, which affects everyone—including the dog.

Of course, positivity is not *always* possible with three kids, misplaced homework, and a dog that wants a walk, but our daily interactions offer a window into empathy, a central theme of this book. Great organizations are able to systematically cultivate empathy, which translates into action, which creates memorable experiences for their guests. This holds true whether you are making breakfast, following up with test results for a patient, or selling a pair of shoes.

Here's another common situation, and one that you are probably very familiar with.

> *It's Saturday, and you've got a lot to do. The first thing on your list is to call your cable company because your internet is down. After being put on hold for fifteen minutes, a representative finally picks up the phone. You explain the problem, and he tries to help you. However, you can't understand what he's saying. You keep asking him to repeat what he wants you to do, and both of you are getting more and more frustrated. In exasperation you ask to speak to his manager. He says the manager is busy, but he'll put you on hold to wait for her. The line is promptly disconnected, so you have to start the process all over again and before you know it, you've wasted three hours trying to get your internet working again before the nightmare ends. You vow to look for another cable service provider as soon as possible, despite feeling deep down that they're all pretty much the same.*

Whether it's not receiving an apology from the barista who gave you a latte when you asked for an espresso, arguing with a clerk when you try to return an item that's clearly broken through no fault of your own, or trying to deal with the cable company, you likely encounter bad service every day. It's frustrating and demoralizing because it seems to be spreading to every type of business. And it's easy to see examples everywhere, especially when they "go viral," as have several eye-opening incidents with airlines over the past couple of years.

In many of these cases, customers distributed videos of poor employee behavior, resulting in negative brand identity for the companies.

These issues are more likely to occur when an organization has not made a commitment to implementing systems that reward exceptional customer experiences. Therefore, the result we see as consumers is mostly disappointing, a "death by a thousand pricks" that has devolved into these negative patterns of behavior. I am not suggesting that just a song and a smile can change the workplace, but there are meaningful, purposeful tactics that can improve how employees and coworkers feel about work and ultimately improve the interactions between any organization and its customers, guests, clients, or patrons.

Take a step back and think about businesses and people who deliver outstanding customer service and how they make you feel when you interact with them. Probably pretty good, right? This isn't exactly a revelation, and trying to understand the framework for developing and building great customer relationships is nothing new. There are a lot of smart people who have written about the value of managing and maintaining customer loyalty, and some of them do it so well that they offer classes (a couple of them are even mentioned in this book). However, this book is focused on attacking the challenge of quality service delivery from a different angle. Namely: as the economy and workforce evolve, and as employees and consumers increasingly interact over the internet and even choose to forgo personal interaction whenever possible, what is the value of delivering great service? And how can empathy translate and even expand in the digital age?

THE TIMES THEY ARE A-CHANGIN'

As the workforce transitions and millennials begin to take a more prominent role in frontline and leadership positions throughout the service economy, the need for understanding and managing quality customer service is compounded. In the past, many organizations in the service sector relied on mentoring and even apprenticeship models to train the next generation. However, both employees' and customers' expectations are quickly making the "old ways" less relevant. Often, I hear clients bemoaning the lack of willingness among new employees for "putting in the time" or "doing the grunt work." While that may or may not be true, organizations must take responsibility for updating their own hiring practices, customer service training, and general workplace culture.

It's time to accept a new paradigm rather than try to force the workforce into the traditional "top-down" management style, which has largely run its course. As one of the leaders profiled in this book, Nick Sarillo, says, "I love that millennials expect more from me. It forces me to think about my actions and be accountable. It forces me to think about work from their perspective."

MILLENNIALS: CHALLENGES AND OPPORTUNITIES

There's no doubt that millennials, the eighty-three million Americans born between the early 1980s and early 2000s (according to commentators, there are no formerly recognized dates for this demographic) have already reshaped parts of the workforce. And this goes well beyond Silicon Valley, where many of them rule the roost. To put their potential future influence in perspective, it helps to compare their cohort size to the baby boomers, who number "only" seventy-five million and have, until now, been the largest and most influential generation in history. (US Census Bureau)

Some people, including a few in this book, argue that "people are individuals" and you can't generalize about generations. They are correct; we are all individuals. However, I also subscribe to the beliefs of researchers Chip Espinoza and Mick Ukleja. In their book *Managing the Millennials: Discover the Core Competencies for Managing Today's Workforce*, they cite generational theory, the idea that each generation is impacted by what is going on in the world around them. They argue that millennials *are* different from previous generations, in large part because of technology and social forces unique at this point in American history.

As millennials begin to rise into management roles and become managers of even younger millennials (as well as Generation Z, the cohort following them), the challenge of helping them understand and value customer service becomes even greater. The reason for this is easy to pinpoint: they, unlike every previous generation in human history, have grown up with the internet. Once upon a time, consumers didn't have the option of sitting in pajamas at a kitchen table, placing an order on a computer and receiving it within one to two days. For those who grew up with the internet, the efficiency and ease of website navigation and product delivery is a very important metric of customer service. They have much less experience with physically walking into a store or place of business and talking to a salesperson before purchasing a product or service. That means they may not be personally familiar with the value and importance that consumers place on positive interpersonal interactions within the service economy. Because it's not something they've been exposed to or experienced, many millennials just don't realize that people are willing to pay more for a product if they receive outstanding customer service face-to-face.

"Technology isn't a tool to just do more work or achieve work–life blending—it's an integral part of the members of this group and working with it has become second nature," Espinoza and Ukleja write: "Millennials are the most-educated and technologically savvy generation ever and arguably a highly sheltered and structured generation. One in three is not Caucasian. One in four comes from a single-parent home. Three in four have working mothers; and in two-parent homes, children get more time with parents than they did twenty-five years ago."[2]

2   Chip Espinoza and Mick Ukleja, *Managing the Millennials: Discover the Core Competencies for Managing Today's Workforce*, (Hoboken, NJ: John Wiley & Sons, 2016), 7.

Compared to every previous generation, their ease with technology makes millennials more dependent on and adept at wielding it; this is one of their many key distinguishing features. It also greatly affects how they view authority and the way they accomplish tasks, which is probably why there is a section about how to work with, manage, and understand millennials in every library and bookstore. You may have heard (and even agree with) some of the common stereotypes; "entitled," "disloyal," "unfocused," and "self-absorbed" were just a few of the words that used to roll around in my head even though two of my three children, who I adore, are millennials.

After reading a number of books—such as *Managing the Millennials*; *Millennials & Management*; and *The Millennial Myth*—I realized that I, as a member of Generation X, had fallen into an echo chamber and succumbed to embracing the negative stereotypes without any real cause. If someone I knew complained about a millennial employee, my brain flitted to all the negative stereotypes I had read on the Web or heard about in conversations. It's exactly what Crystal Kadakia (a millennial herself) writes about in her book, *The Millennial Myth: Transforming Misunderstanding into Workplace Breakthroughs:*

> Two different worlds collided: the world of the distinguished expert and the world of the digital influencer. As social media's two-way information flow grew at an enormous rate post-2000, the distinctly negative perception won out, because, frankly, that is what made headlines. . . . In contrast, while every generation has dealt with complaints, gen X and boomers didn't have such a variety of high-volume, fast-paced sources of vocal discontent to contend with when they were coming of age.[3]

3   Crystal Kadakia, *The Millennial Myth*, (Oakland, CA: Berrett-Koehler Publishers, Inc., 2017), 3.

Of course, it never occurred to me that technology was amplifying the negative views, and I hadn't even considered what generations previous to mine would have thought of me and my peers had the internet been available.

What's important for our purpose is to understand that the companies that offer outstanding service have aligned their management structure, vision, and other "best practices" with the values of the millennial generation. All the organizations in this book have strong visions and values, whether they were established at the very beginning, like they were at Zingerman's, or developed organically, like they have at Zappos. It's no coincidence that those businesses, as well as all the others covered in this book, appeal to members of the current generation—people who value meaning at work in the same way the baby boomers valued professional identity.

Espinoza and Ukleja argue that, contrary to popular opinion, unlocking the potential of millennials really isn't that complicated. "You have to help millennials find a reason to care," they advise. "They are the easiest of the workforce to motivate once you have helped them find meaning in what they do. You keep them motivated by letting them see how what they do matters. They thrive in an atmosphere of change—not because of change itself, but because they get to put their mark on the future."[4]

This idea that "finding meaning" in work is important for this generation is also expressed by Lee Caraher in her book, *Millennials & Management: The Essential Guide to Making It Work at Work*. In it, she has prescriptive advice for managers who want to get the best work out of their millennial employees:

---

4   Espinoza and Ukleja, *Managing the Millennials*, 157.

[Managers] should be able to answer these questions:

1. This job exists to:
2. *My* job is to make sure that:
3. If I wasn't here, this is what wouldn't happen:
    That last step, the individual's immediate picture—why "I" make a difference—is critical. It may seem excessive, I know, but if people understand their purpose within the bigger vision, if they can tie their day-to-day work to making a difference, then work goes a bit more smoother and more efficiently, with better output and good morale all the way around.[5]

Whether common characteristics of the millennial generation are labeled "core competencies" or "intrinsic values," they significantly affect the workplace. Managers who want to engage this generation must recognize that giving clear, unambiguous instruction and feedback is as essential as realizing that the old "command and control" hierarchy is not a good fit for people who grew up Googling answers on a computer instead of asking an authority figure. Understanding that there truly are differences in the way this generation works and interacts compared to previous ones also means acknowledging that different techniques to teach, nurture, and manage them are required compared to earlier generations, whether they are working in a hospital or a hotel.

Let's face it: for all the benefits technology brings, hospitality as we have defined it is not in the mix. This means ongoing, purposeful customer service training is required. Whether they're working in an independent pizza parlor or an organization of eighty thousand employees, millennials have to learn to appreciate the value of hospitality

---

5 Lee Caraher, *Millennials & Management: The Essential Guide to Making It Work at Work*, (Brookline, MA: Bibliomotion, Inc., 2015), 47.

without relying on the older practices of mentoring and apprenticeship, a change that is only going to become more pronounced as they rise to leadership positions throughout the service economy. This is a problem because the new workforce has less exposure to the customer's need to be recognized, appreciated, and respected, especially given the challenges posed by technology when it comes to personal interactions.

Most best-in-class organizations in this book understand that younger employees are less likely to have an inherent understanding of how to manage direct relationships over time. This means that in addition to accepting the value of efficient product delivery, businesses must teach their employees communication and relationship-building. (As the businesses profiled in this book have done, and done well.)

Of course, many service sector organizations have a training program of some kind, but new employees do not necessarily have the same tools at their disposal to establish a culture of exceptional service that previous generations had. At the same time that there's been an increase in formal customer service training programs in most companies, there has also been a decrease in what I'd call "informal" customer service training. In the past, experienced employees passed their knowledge to the next generation of workers, so even after the week or two of training ended, there was still plenty of on-the-job instruction. Although many factors have contributed to the decrease in informal training, the consequences will continue to be felt for years due to this large demographic switch.

All of which is to say, the organizations that can harness the energy of millennials and master this challenge will increase customer loyalty and profits.

ACCOUNTABILITY: WHERE THE RUBBER HITS THE ROAD

Throughout the examples in this book, we will see the motivations and associated habits of great leaders. Each of them has a unique story, but they all share certain common traits. In the end, there are five characteristics that seem to weave in and out of each story: authenticity, accountability, culture, community, and vision. These values manifest themselves in hiring practices, training routines, performance reviews, corporate communication, and beyond.

Not all of these traits are easily mastered, however, as Susan Salgado, the hospitality consultant, explains, "Leadership is where the rubber hits the road, and where we see the most clients struggling with it is in accountability. They've got a vision of what they want the customer experience to look and feel like, but they are not good at holding people accountable to that." It's not surprising to hear that accountability is important, but, as you will read throughout the book, these leaders seem to hold themselves to a higher standard of accountability than others I have met. They recognize that vision alone is not an adequate substitute for consistent behaviors that support their vision.

One story that comes to mind from the book is from Richard Coraine, chief of staff at Union Square Hospitality Group, one of the country's largest and most acclaimed restaurant groups. He likens accountability to cleaning a kitchen. You tell an employee to clean the kitchen, and the dedicated employee thinks he's done an excellent job. Then, you run your finger under the counter and find it dirty and wonder why the employee thought the kitchen was clean when it obviously wasn't. But, you, the manager, did not explain to the employee what you meant by a "clean" kitchen at the outset. As a result, you are disappointed, the employee is frustrated, and the kitchen is not clean. Who is to blame?

Great leadership requires a consistent embrace of behavior that begins and ends with accountability. Especially in an age where younger employees are less likely to trust authority and are looking for a collaborative work environment, it is imperative that leaders consistently deliver authenticity and accountability in the workplace. As you will read in example after example, when employees feel like there is meaning and accountability throughout the organization, they will deliver exceptional service to customers.

YOU NEED THE RIGHT TOOLS

Some businesses in the hospitality sector, including hotels, restaurants, and coffee shops, have developed a methodical, data-driven structure to the steps of service in order to retain customers and increase profits. You as the customer don't realize any of this; all you know is that these businesses deliver memorable experiences not just occasionally but all the time. They're the places you come back to again and again because you know you'll experience excellence, no matter where or what time of day you arrive. Many of these tools have existed since the first days of the modern restaurant 250 years ago, when the first restaurants were called *Maisons de Santé* or "Houses of Health" in Paris. However they developed, they continue to play a large role in satisfying you as a customer.

I believe that harnessing the tools of the hospitality sector and applying them purposefully to other aspects of the service economy, such as medical and financial institutions, online retailers, and telecoms, will not only help companies develop formal training practices but also lead to a return on investment (ROI) with increased profits.

This book will begin by exploring the origins of customer service. It will then review some of the key components and models of quality service delivery, and then it will discuss the best practices with industry leaders throughout the service economy. You will read about how great organizations hire the right employees for their culture, motivate and train their staff, and set up structures to ensure great service, whether they employ thousands of people worldwide or a few hundred in suburban Chicago. You'll see how investments in training have paid off with increased loyalty, revenue growth, and, ultimately, increased profitability.

As Susan Salgado puts it, "It's not like it costs money to do this. We're talking about how we treat people, and it's not necessarily about throwing free stuff at them. It's not going to decrease your productivity. In fact, you can increase productivity significantly because you'll have fewer customer complaints you'll have to dig your way out of." In the end, leading through hospitality is a commonsense formula for success and offers ways for making all of us smile just a bit more often.

UNDERSTANDING THE BASICS

Isn't it wonderful to find a product you love? When I think about it, the mattress I'm currently using is spectacular and well worth the premium I paid for a good night's sleep. However, after about a year, I started noticing some inconsistencies in the structure of the product. Some parts felt worn and uneven and I wasn't sleeping as soundly, so I called the store where I purchased the mattress to discuss the issue. Prior to the call, I found the receipt and noticed it had a ten-year warranty that said I was entitled to a full replacement if the mattress was defective, which it seemed to be. However, after speaking with a young and inexperienced salesperson, I could immediately tell that resolving my problem wasn't going to be easy. In fact, it took multiple calls over several weeks before the company finally accepted responsibility for the product failure. Even though I got what I wanted (and was entitled to), by the end of the ordeal I wasn't relieved or thankful. I was extremely irritated.

Here's how this example should be illustrative for every company in the service economy, including yours. The hassle of taking time out of my day to repeatedly deal with the matter soured me on the company to such an extent that I will never purchase a similar mattress again *even though it is by far the best one I've ever had.* While this is a simple example, it highlights the reality that the "best in class" service providers have already figured out: wonderful products are nothing without exceptional service.

HOSPITALITY LEADING THE WAY

Unlike many other industries, the hospitality industry is built on the relationship between an organization—whether a restaurant, hotel, or even a casino   and its target customer. Moreover, hospitality businesses have had to focus on customer service for years to retain and broaden their customer base. As a result, these organizations have developed significant systems and points of service that not only differentiate them from each other but also from the rest of the service economy.

In many cases, exceptional customer service providers in the hospitality industry must navigate constant internal physical and interpersonal constraints while simultaneously managing the expectations of their customers. The only way hospitality companies have been able to meet high expectations is to create standardized, purposeful customer service training that continues every day for as long as the company is in business. This is one of the many philosophies you will encounter throughout this book. Great organizations do not stop after the initial training is over; success is an ongoing, iterative process that is expensive initially but pays off tenfold over the long haul by developing and then keeping loyal customers.

For example, at Lettuce Entertain You Enterprises, a 150-venue restaurant group profiled in this book, there is a daily staff meeting before each meal service. Expectations for the day are outlined, VIP customers identified, new menu items discussed, and so on. This daily, ten-minute, customer service training session happens at every Lettuce Entertainment restaurant, in more or less the same way, every day, across the country.

Fortunately for the rest of us, the standards and practices highlighted in this book can benefit organizations beyond the hospitality sector. The companies profiled in this book, such as Lettuce Entertain You, Union Square Hospitality Group, and Hyatt, are industry leaders and have been for a long time, but their methods are universal. These companies have developed sophisticated tools to ensure that each of their customers feel valued and appreciated, but these tools can be adopted by any company that wants to improve their customer service.

Some might argue that as technology streamlines our relationship to products, hospitality is less relevant, but I think the reverse is true. In our impersonal world, our natural need for recognition and appreciation makes the need for *empathy* and *action* that much more critical. Loyal customers are profit-driving customers. Loyal customers spend more over time and require little, if any, incentives to return again and again for the same quality and the same service. That's why my experience with the mattress is so illustrative. If the company had solved my problem after the first phone call, they would have earned a customer for life instead of losing one.

Through a series of conversations and case studies, we'll discuss some time-proven best practices from hospitality organizations and other industries within the service sector. Some of these studies focus on the company's internal customers—their employees—and demonstrate the value of training and building a culture around hospitality. Other studies review the relationship between consumers and providers to explain the intrinsic connection between long-term loyalty and profit. To help you realize these goals, the book outlines purposeful management strategies that emphasize the importance of leveraging hospitality training throughout the service economy, especially at a time when the dynamics of the workforce are changing quickly and radically.

The challenges of today will only intensify over the coming years as an increasing number of baby boomers and other more experienced employees leave the workforce. Most people (but not all, as you will see) agree that the generation currently entering the workforce arrives with different expectations, and employers can either try and fight the new reality or adapt and improve, especially when it comes to quality service delivery. But despite what you may have heard—or experienced—this *is* an exciting time. Changes in the workplace and customer expectations are evolving quickly, and the stories in this book reveal worthwhile ideas—some simple, some complex—about how to improve workplace culture and, ultimately, deliver meaning to employees and customers alike.

PRODUCTS AND SERVICES

In order to clearly understand the concepts in this book, it's important to distinguish between "products" and "services," especially because the transition to a more service-based economy has created such dramatic shifts in the consumer landscape. The definition of "product" is pretty straightforward: it's something that can be inventoried, patented, and even displayed: anything from a hotel room or a pair of shoes to an online accounting service or a sticker. All mass-produced products are designed to be consistent and are defined by price, promotions, placement, and other tangible factors.

"Services," on the other hand, are less easily defined because they cannot be inventoried and are inconsistent and fleeting. The waiter bringing your coffee, the housekeeper cleaning your hotel room, and the airline representative rebooking your flight all offer services, which create both challenges and opportunities. Organizations with high-quality customer service recognize the difference between their products and their associated services. Those that excel and keep your loyalty despite unforeseen problems mitigate many of the challenges inherent in the products by acting with empathy during the service encounter.

A BRIEF HISTORY LESSON

Before we dig into the interviews and case studies, some background is in order. Our best chance of understanding the challenges service providers face today, as well as those they will face in the future, is to examine the not-so-distant past. The transition from pre- to post-industrial times necessitated a new approach to customer service, and it has been continually evolving ever since, even though some key lessons have been either hard-fought or ignored.

In the interest of brevity, let's focus on a representative example of many of the changes that have occurred over the past century: Bell Labs. A key player in the products and services industry, the company formed in 1925, when four thousand scientists and researchers from Western Electric Company and the American Telephone & Telegraph Company (AT&T) were pulled into a new company: Bell Telephone Laboratories. Like Apple or Google in Silicon Valley today, Bell Labs was considered the premier tech company in the country and was as influential in the psyche of the American consumer. Bell Labs was revolutionary for its day, servicing such entities as the telephone company and the US Government. Like Tesla, Amazon, and scores of other contemporary companies, Bell Labs spent money, time, and energy testing and developing new products, ranging from the transistor to the Unix operating system. That dedication to research and development paid off, and, beginning in 1937, the company was awarded eight Nobel Prizes over a seventy-seven-year period. However, creating the technology for the transistor (Nobel Prize awarded in 1956) is one thing; ensuring that the product will work when mass-produced is another. Luckily, by that time, a system had been developed to do just that.

The formal recognition that *quality* was an important factor in production began in the 1920s, when Walter Shewhart, an American physicist and statistician commonly known as the "father of statistical quality control," identified the need to control the quality of industrial products. He invented an elaborate system that introduced tracking charts to monitor quality in mass production, and then named the concept "statistical process control." The process was later adopted by Bell Labs as a way to ensure that their mass-produced telephone products and consumer goods were meeting company standards. In fact, Shewhart's methods were considered so sound that they were later implemented in weapons production during World War II.

Unfortunately for American consumers and businesses, the lessons learned before the war about tracking service quality were largely forgotten after it. There was a general and unquestioned sense that America's superior ingenuity and systems were simply better than their foreign competitors and did not require any systemized quality control. In contrast, the Japanese, during their post-World War II reconstruction, realized how important quality was to the success of a product, and they famously adopted the theories developed and pitched to them by two Westerners, W. Edwards Deming and Joseph Juran, in the 1950s.

Both Deming and Juran believed that the majority of product defects were caused by poor management, not inept line workers, whom Americans usually blamed. Additionally, the two men thought implementing superior quality control processes while a product was being made was a far better use of resources than hiring a team of inspectors to find and assess flaws afterward. This sounds like a no-brainer now, but it was a revolutionary idea for its time. Deming and Juran convinced Japanese business leaders that if workers were given the right tools and the responsibility for making sure things were done correctly, quality would improve and there would be no need to hire teams of inspectors after the product was made. As you probably know, their argument was a persuasive one. Beginning in the 1960s, their theories strongly influenced Japanese manufacturers from Toyota to Sony and helped the "Made in Japan" phrase signify consistent, reliable products, whether a consumer was buying a Toyota car or a Sony Walkman.

While the Japanese were reorganizing their manufacturing processes around Deming and Juran's theories, few American entrepreneurs similarly recognized the importance of structuring a company around consistently delivering a quality product. In general, American manufacturing took a step backward and focused on a "top-down," hierarchical management style, where managers outlined expectations and demanded results, with an emphasis on short-term financial gain.

In fact, even now—in a climate where there are extraordinary demands on profitability—many organizations still have this mentality baked into their culture. For many years, the American automotive industry was a good example of this shortsighted attitude. It's no coincidence that the industry is now a shadow of what it once was. Ignoring quality during previous decades adversely affected sales, and this choice still affects the industry's reputation today. Consistent progress is being made in the American auto industry, but the memories linger.

THE DAWN OF CUSTOMER SERVICE IN AMERICA

In the nineteenth and twentieth centuries, urbanization expanded in the United States at a remarkable rate, from one out of four Americans living in cities in the 1870s, to two out three Americans in the 1960s. As a result, the need for services rather than goods also increased exponentially, and American companies began to recognize the significance of the shift from a manufacturing-based economy to one that was (and remains) service-driven. This shift in the economic landscape led companies to rethink their organizational approach—not to mention that at that point, the Japanese manufacturing success story was a clearly defined marker for success. Finally, American companies also began to heed Deming and Juran's advice and rethink their organizational structures, since it was becoming glaringly obvious that the relationship between managers and workers directly affected outcomes such as job productivity, job satisfaction, and employee retention. During the 1990s, companies realized it wasn't enough to just mass produce consistent products. They also needed a more holistic approach, with the entire organization acting as one team to ensure consistent products and offering great customer service to complement them.

Even though it may be hard to believe, the concept of "quality customer service" has only existed for about forty years. As companies realized it wasn't good enough to simply engineer a good product, the best organizations recognized that offering quality services, or the idea that the organization would meet or beat customer expectations and remain economically competitive, would distinguish themselves from their competitors. This opened up a whole new conceptualization of the relationship between businesses and their consumers and ultimately forced companies to rethink their internal and external relationships. Relationships between managers and line employees, managers and the company culture, and the company and the public were seen as equal parts of a triad.

This being the case, some creative business leaders from firms as large as Hyatt Hotels Corporation and as small as Zingerman's Delicatessen in Ann Arbor, Michigan, understood that in order to excel they had to make sure that employees had the right tools and training to communicate with their customers in a different way. At an early stage, they figured out that the emotional connection between the customer and the brand was the key to differentiating themselves from the competition. Effectively, these companies reimagined customer service as a more emotional connection between provider and consumer.

Take Steve Hindy, who revolutionized the craft beer industry through his company, Brooklyn Brewery. Though he had no hospitality background, he inherently understood the importance of training his sales team and creating a culture around the brewery that has sustained his business from 1988 to today. Although he focused on building brand loyalty through a great product, he quickly realized that customer service could be a defining characteristic of a great company. Steve Hindy is not alone in this belief, as you will see.

MEETING RISING EXPECTATIONS

As customer service delivery became more sophisticated and more American businesses sought to build loyalty by offering better service delivery, consumers developed higher expectations about the brands themselves, which, in turn, directly affected brand identity. The growing challenge for companies was to ensure that there was no gap between the consumer's expectation and the company's product and delivery (or, if a gap occurred, it was as small as possible). While that might sound intuitive today, it was still a work in progress less than thirty years ago. (And even today, as my earlier example about the nonresponsive mattress company made abundantly clear, it is still a work in progress.) If anything, a kind of arms race ensued as companies began to work harder and harder to exceed expectations, knowing a disconnect between their brands and their service delivery could be disastrous.

To demonstrate what this means, let's think about airline travel. After scouring the internet and spending hundreds of dollars on an airline ticket, the average flyer knows the flight won't necessarily be relaxing or pleasant, but she does expect it will take off and land at approximately the prescribed time. However, if there is an extended delay, she will become annoyed, and it becomes the responsibility of the airline to recognize and apologize for the inconvenience, even in cases when it's beyond the airline's control. If an airline does not have a service recovery protocol in place, the airline will lose customers and tarnish its image; the damage to the airline's brand will be long-lasting and expensive. What to do? For just a small cost, the airline can mitigate the gap between expectations and reality by offering an incentive or compensation for the delay (free snack, or travel voucher with compensation determined by the length and severity of the delay). Equally important, the airline can make sure the employees are well trained to handle unexpected flight delays with empathy and a smile rather than apathy and a snarl. All of us constantly reevaluate brand choice based on the gap between expectation and reality. If the airline meets our expectations, or comes close to meeting them, we will fly with them again. If they fail to meet our basic expectations, we will be a lot less likely to.

Organizations with strong service recognize that individual consumers have an established "zone of tolerance," a term defined as "the range of customer perceptions of a service between desired and minimum acceptable standards."[6] In essence it is the range of service performance that a customer considers satisfactory. One solution organizations have adopted to address individual zones of tolerance occurs at the onset of the service experience. It is based on the one-on-one relationship between an individual company employee and the

---

6 Zeithami, Valarie, Berry, Leonard, Parasuraman, A. "Communication and Control Processes in the Delivery of Service Quality." Journal of Marketing, Vol. 52, Issue 2, 35-48. 4/1988.

customer. One familiar image we have of this type of relationship is expressed in TV commercials advertising financial services consulting. Picture an investment advisor and her clients: as the clients confess their different dreams—such as to retire early, to send their children to college, or to start a business—the smiling advisor listens to each person individually and offers sage advice to all of them.

The goal of the commercial is to demonstrate the value of strong relationships in personal finance, and it does this by showing how each and every person is valued by the company, no matter how small or large her portfolio. Even if this isn't true, the *message* of caring and empathy resonates and is the reason this individualized approach works and with appropriate training can be a successful customer service model.

Unfortunately, conveying this message is never as simple as we would like it to be. Most organizations struggle for a variety of reasons with delivering on the promise of exceptional service. One of the biggest is a lack of accountable, consistent leadership that, in turn, drives the focus on exceptional service.

In fact, consistency is probably the most important aspect of quality customer service delivery. Many companies spend an enormous amount of time and resources trying to ensure their brand identity remains consistent through advertising, slogans, and even mission statements, but give relatively little thought to the consumer's direct interaction with that same brand, a significant disconnect between the importance of product *and* service. The value of ongoing training that emphasizes an appreciation and understanding of outstanding service cannot be underestimated. Even in the best cases, long-term employees can become jaded over time, forgetting or dismissing the brand promise for expediency.

Over the next nine chapters, you will be introduced to some exceptional leaders. They have all developed tools that have reshaped the organizational landscape of their companies. As you will see, this process often starts with hiring and training, but that merely scratches the surface. Whether consciously or not, they have embraced the true meaning of hospitality to help their organizations frame their core vision and values. The results provide insight on new ways to think about every aspect of the employee experience. In turn, these leaders have found that their organizations are rewarded tenfold with exceptionally loyal employees, customers, and, ultimately, more efficient and profitable business models. That's a recipe for success!

THE EVANGELISTS

Ari Weinzweig	Nick Sarillo	Paul Spiegelman
(Zingerman's Delicatessen)	*(Nick's Pizza & Pub)*	*(BerylHealth)*

Passionate about their vision and values and methodical about how they implement them, these three leaders practice what they preach. They strive to make work meaningful and society better, and they are certain that treating employees and customers well leads to financial success.

While they approach their roles as leaders with the same level of commitment and attention to detail, each has taken his own path in molding the infrastructure of his organization. Additionally, they actively send their message out into the wider community through well-designed training programs (Ari and Nick) and purposeful podcasting (Paul).

CHAPTER 1

ZINGERMAN'S:
LASER-FOCUSED ON CUSTOMER SERVICE

"I think that if people don't believe that customer service is a critical thing, then they're going to do as little as possible, and then it's going to be only done as a tactical tool, which is sort of like the person who eats a half dessert instead of a whole dessert, and that's their tactical tool to get in shape. So it's not bad, but it's not going to create a meaningful life." —**ARI WEINZWEIG**

I'LL TAKE A SIDE OF CUSTOMER SERVICE, PLEASE

If you like good food and you live in Ann Arbor, Michigan, you already know all about Zingerman's Delicatessen, which is as much of an institution as its neighbor, the University of Michigan. You've probably started at least one day with their roasted coffee along with a freshly baked cinnamon roll. Or maybe you've stopped by the deli for a #48, Binny's Brooklyn Reuben, a side of Alterna Slaw, and a Magic Brownie. At night, you may have eaten at Zingerman's Roadhouse restaurant, which offers the company's unique spin on comfort food, or stopped by Zingerman's Creamery to bring home a pint of gelato, fresh mozzarella, and Detroit Street Brick Cheese.

It all started back in the early '80s, when Paul Saginaw and Ari

Weinzweig became friends. The two met at a restaurant after Ari graduated from the University of Michigan; Saginaw was the manager and Ari was the dishwasher. As their friendship evolved, they decided to band together and open a deli in an old brick building in a part of Ann Arbor called Kerrytown. In 1982, Zingerman's was born.

Since then, Zingerman's has come to comprise a diverse community of businesses that includes everything from the deli itself to a candy manufacturer and Korean restaurant. Much has already been written about Zingerman's. Bo Burlingham dubbed it "The Coolest Small Company in America" in a 2003 article in *Inc.* magazine, and Micheline Maynard of the *New York Times* wrote an article titled "The Corner Deli that Dared to Break Out of the Neighborhood" in 2007, Zingerman's twenty-fifth anniversary.

Ari is an author in his own right, and has written multiple books and pamphlets explaining Zingerman's business philosophy. Available through Zingerman's Press, the titles are diverse and range from the fifty-two-page pamphlet *Bottom Line Change: Zingerman's Recipe for Effective Organizational Change* to full books such as *Zingerman's Guide to Good Leading Part 4: A Lapsed Anarchist's Approach to the Power of Beliefs in Business* (there are also parts 1 to 3) and my favorite, *Zingerman's Guide to Giving Great Service.*

In addition to its mission and guiding principles, another feature that defines Zingerman's is its decision to develop new, independent businesses rather than franchise successful ones. Firmly rooted in Ann Arbor, each new business is operated by one or more managing partners who not only run the business but also share ownership. Annual revenue companywide is now about $62 million—a far cry from the early days at the deli.

However, not all of the businesses under the Zingerman's umbrella revolve around retail. ZingTrain, their customer service and leadership training company, hosts seminars in Ann Arbor and on-site around the country. It's run by Maggie Bayless, who worked in the deli while getting her MBA at Michigan in the late 1980s. Asked why she got involved with ZingTrain, she says she admired its focus on customer service.

"After graduation, I stayed in touch with Ari and Paul and watched how they worked to build an organizational culture that focused on service not only to paying customers but also to staff and each other," she says. "I didn't find that approach to service, or to leadership, in any of the companies where I worked post-MBA. So in 1994 I saw an opportunity to bring my passion for training back to Zingerman's—to both improve the quality of internal training and also to offer outside organizations an inside look at how Zingerman's does business. From the beginning, customer service training was the number one topic that ZingTrain clients have been looking for."

GUIDING PRINCIPLES

At some companies, the mission statement and guiding principles (if they exist) may be in the employee handbook, but they are definitely not ingrained in the company's culture. Not so at Zingerman's, where the guiding principles inspire day-to-day decisions as well as future ones. They are the foundation of how employees relate to one another, their customers, suppliers, and the greater Ann Arbor community.

As a cofounder of Zingerman's, Ari has played a huge role in establishing, nurturing, and growing its customer service philosophy. A self-described "lapsed anarchist," he is deeply passionate when he speaks about customer service, which is as essential to Zingerman's identity as a pastrami sandwich from the deli. This isn't just lip service.

Unlike most companies, which only consider a financial bottom line, Zingerman's has three bottom lines: Great Food, Great Service, and Great Finance.

Customers don't accidentally have a good experience at Zingerman's. Customer service is woven into the fabric of the company, as the text from bottom line number 2, below, shows.

"Our business exists only because of customers who spend their money on our products. The customer is the only reason we are here. Consequently, the customer is never an interruption. Without those customers, there would be no Zingerman's and no jobs. Consequently, the customer always comes first."

One morning, during a busy breakfast at the Roadhouse, Ari and I spoke about all this. The room was filled with people of all ages and occupations, from millennials with babies and people in suits to older couples enjoying a cup of coffee. Over the chatter from patrons and servers, Ari explained Zingerman's customer service philosophy.

"Customer service has been a bottom line, a literally, overtly stated bottom line for us, for twenty-seven years. We said in the mid-'90s that we have *three* bottom lines. And one of the reasons that we did that was because we decided that for us customer service was an end in and of itself. It wasn't just a tactical step."

He took a sip of tea and continued.

"For us it's a core piece of everything. And I think really that's why we did it, but I think it extends to people's lives everywhere because it's a mindset around your existence in the world."

Before we discuss exactly *how* Zingerman's delivers on the promise of meeting and exceeding customers' expectations, it's essential to understand a bit more about the philosophy of the company and why it has garnered so much national attention.

To begin with, for Ari and everyone else at Zingerman's, "Great Service" is not just one of three bottom lines: it's also the second of eight guiding principles, all of which are spelled out on the company's website and in its printed literature. Along with the company's mission statement and bottom lines, its guiding principles seem to be engraved on Ari's heart, holding him accountable not only to Zingerman's customers but also to its employees, from the bus girl to the managing partners.

These guiding principles weave together a very particular culture. And, as you can see, they are as enthusiastic as the people who work there:

1. Great Food!
2. Great Service!
3. A Great Place to Shop and Eat!
4. Solid Profits!
5. A Great Place to Work!
6. Strong Relationships!
7. A Place to Learn!
8. An Active Part of Our Community!

Reading guiding principle number 2, "Great Service!," it's easy to be cynical. You've probably heard something like it before:

We go the x-tra mile, giving exceptional service to each guest. We are committed to giving great service—meeting the guests' expectations and then exceeding them. Great service like this is at the core of the Zingerman's Experience. Our guests always leave with a sense of wonderment at how we have gone out of our way to make their experience at Zingerman's a rewarding one.

If you've just done a mental eye roll, I don't blame you. Pretty much every business claims to "go the extra mile" and "care" about your experience, even cable companies and airlines. However, in talking with Ari it's very clear that these are not just empty words. He emphatically believes that he and his team not only need to meet customers' expectations, but continually exceed them before, during and after the sale. They do this in myriad ways. One small example training employees to look people in the eye or engage verbally, depending upon how far from the customer they're standing.

"Our job is to increase expectations," says Ari. "Don't you have higher expectations of yourself than you used to? Everybody that's growing is increasing their expectations. It's a good problem."

This belief is reflected in the description of Zingerman's second guiding principle:

> Customer satisfaction is the fuel that stokes the Zingerman's fire. If our guests aren't happy, we're not happy. To this end, we consistently go the x-tra mile—literally and figuratively—for our guests. The customer is never an interruption in our day. We welcome feedback of all sorts. We constantly reevaluate our performance to better accommodate our customers. Our goal is to have our guests leave happy. Each of us takes full responsibility for making our guest's experience an enjoyable one before, during, and after the sale.

You may be thinking, as I was, "Nice words. But how does that work in a concrete way?" Well, here's how: Zingerman's has an internal process to evaluate complaints and compliments using "Code Red" and "Code Green" forms. Employees write a Code Green when they receive a compliment or hear another employee receiving one. In contrast, employees write a Code Red when there is a complaint of any kind. If there's a Code Red, the employee explains what the issue was and how it was resolved. And the issue is almost always resolved. If the line employee and managers can't "make it right," they'll go up the chain until they find a managing partner.

Ari admits there have been a few people over the years who have taken advantage of Zingerman's willingness to do just about anything to make a customer happy, but the vast majority don't. Most people are just grateful that someone cared enough to listen to their complaint and apologize, before fixing the problem.

Ari smiled when I told him that I thought that the next part of guiding principle number 2, giving great service is an "honorable profession," was unique.

"One of the biggest things that we do is to get the message across that service is honorable because if you're taking flak from your friends and family, you can do it, but it's very difficult to stay grounded and rooted. My mother, ten years after we were open, she was still asking me when I was going to go to law school." He pauses and looks me straight in the eye. "I'm not exaggerating."

This is a far cry from the stereotypical image of a service-oriented job. Consider, say, a call center, where customer service representatives are near the bottom of the hierarchy, or a fine restaurant where dish washers, busboys, and waitstaff are treated as easily interchangeable, expendable assets. That's why Ari says that this belief is hard for some people to grasp when he teaches customer service seminars through ZingTrain.

"People have the belief that service is a terrible thing to have to do. If you're a doctor, and you worked your ass off for literally fifteen to twenty years to get to your job, and you've been taught that puts you at the top of the hierarchy, and now some adviser comes in and goes, 'No, she's a bus girl and you should be nice to her.' That belief is not congruent in your mind."

Everyone, he says, is influenced by the people around them. Therefore, if managers and other leaders only *say* the right things, sooner or later what they truly believe, that the people dealing with the customers aren't as important as the managers, or that striving for good service is "a crock," then these beliefs will permeate the organization no matter what the mission statement says. Another part of guiding principle number 2 reads:

> We give great service to each other as well as to our guests. We
> provide the same level of service to our peers as we do our guests.
> We are polite, supportive, considerate, superb listeners, and always
> willing to go the x-tra mile for each other.

This guiding principle, that serving peers within an organization
is as important as serving customers, flows out of "servant leadership"
philosophy and practices. First outlined in an essay by Robert Greenleaf
in 1970 and then expanded into the book *Servant Leadership: A Journey
into the Nature of Legitimate Power and Greatness* in 1977, the basic
idea of "servant leadership" is that staff will give no better service to
customers than managers give to staff and managers will give no better
service to staff than owners give to managers.

In this way, it becomes incumbent on the leadership to give their
employees and customers outstanding service. On a normal day at
Zingerman's, this might manifest itself by a manager asking the sandwich makers if they would like a cold drink, or for Ari to pour water
for customers himself when the Roadhouse is packed.

This concept is taken very seriously throughout the organization.
In a traditional company, the onus of customer service is on those at
the lowest level of the hierarchy. Servant leadership turns that upside
down, because the higher you rise in the hierarchy, the more customers
you have and the greater your responsibility for giving outstanding
customer service to *everyone*.

That's not all. Although it's not an official Zingerman's guiding
principle, the idea that everyone is an individual lies at the heart of
Ari's personal philosophy and Zingerman's approach to customer service inside and outside the organization. It's impossible to convey how
passionate he is about this topic. Indeed, he believes it is "demeaning,"

"dehumanizing," and "counterproductive" not to consider everyone as an individual.

"I think every customer is different and every employee is different. And every customer is different every day, and every employee is different every day, so it's like a kaleidoscope. Most times the same customer doesn't even want the same thing at two different times of the day."

BELIEFS ABOUT GIVING EXCELLENT SERVICE

Not only do Ari's books delve into the power of beliefs in business, his conversations do too. And he is passionate about them. He's established what he calls a "self-fulfilling belief cycle," which affects everything from the ground up. During our meeting, he draws a picture of it: a circle with arrows going around. That's why he is so certain that delivering outstanding customer service increases the financial bottom line, even though he doesn't have hard data to prove it (apart from the company's growth and success over the years).

Asked whether he feels there's a law of diminishing returns when it comes to giving outstanding service, he shakes his head. "I don't think so. If you believe there is a law of diminishing returns, you will find evidence to show that it's not worth it. I don't believe it; I think that it increases one's energy to learn, I believe that it's more fun, and I believe if we're not getting better, we're getting worse, and there's one thousand other people that would be happy to have our customers."

Making guiding principle number 2 a concrete reality takes hard work—a lot of it. Zingerman's has a ninety-day orientation that blends classroom and shift training, with continuing training for the entire time an employee works there, as well as clearly defined expectations for each position, with recognition and rewards when employees succeed. Additionally, like many companies, there are also formal performance reviews plus on-shift feedback and periodic conversations with managers.

In an as-yet unpublished essay he shared with me, Ari writes about the best way to give feedback. After talking with him, it's not at all surprising that he sees it as a two-way street, as something in which employees and managers equally participate: the former by creating a personal vision of where he or she wants to be in a year, and the latter by helping the employee realize that vision.

He summarized his perspective like this:

"If our work as leaders is a lot about helping everyone here figure out what their dreams are and then successfully go after getting them to be a reality, then inside-outing the approach to performance reviews—which everyone believes in but hardly anyone actually loves doing—could be a big piece of making that happen. [The essay] is based on my belief in each individual's ability to get to greatness, in the power of visioning, and the assumption that one of our main responsibilities as leaders is to help every one of us live their dreams with ever greater efficacy."

THOUGHTS ABOUT THE FUTURE OF CUSTOMER SERVICE

No one knows what the future will bring to any industry. Of course, new technology will continue to usher in changes. Like many restaurants, Zingerman's Roadhouse now texts people when their table is ready, for example. But Ari believes the result of outstanding service—"a guest having a great experience"—is one thing that won't change. The secret, he says, is for the servers to observe their customers carefully to understand what they want.

Ari says many organizations don't train their staff to take cues from the customers to find out what they want at that particular moment. Zingerman's does. So, even if Roadhouse servers *could* talk to customers at length about the food—its origin, processing, and history—they won't if a customer seems to be in a hurry or just plain hungry.

He looks around the room and spots a table of what looks like four students eating breakfast. "A lot of people get in trouble because they're not seeing what the individual customer wants. If you say, 'This is what customers want,' you're already doomed."

Looking at one of the young men at the table, he continues. "If I'm going by his body language, what that guy wants now is to be left alone and chat casually and take forever to eat his breakfast. But later today he might want total efficiency, no conversation, completely on the fly. So if you don't honor that his situations have altered and you can't pick that up from his tone of voice and his body language, you're going to completely misserve him."

The way Zingerman's has reacted to the gluten-free trend offers a revealing example of how it responds to its customers while staying true to its mission. While they sell products that are gluten-free, they know it's not their niche, so they haven't tried to compete with the bakeries in that market.

"We're not a gluten free-bakery, and we're not going into it. It needs to be somebody who's super passionate about gluten-free baking, not somebody who doesn't care about it but is trying to do it to get people's sale. It doesn't mean we can't sell other things that are gluten-free or try to do what we do; we just try to find things that are naturally gluten-free."

MILLENNIALS ARE JUST LIKE US

In the introduction to this book, I discussed some of the research on millennials that argues that they differ from previous generations. Given Ari's philosophy—that everyone is an individual—it isn't surprising that he not only vehemently disagrees with that premise but seems offended by it.

"First of all, I don't believe you can assign a characteristic to ten million people. It doesn't make any sense any more than saying women can't or women can do something. This is a core thing for me. The belief that people can assign characteristics makes no sense."

"If you believe millennials are lazy and unproductive and difficult to work with, how will you treat them? You'll treat them with weird energy and you won't really engage them. Then what do they believe? They believe work sucks and you're a jerk. Then how do they work? Badly, and you say, 'See, they're terrible.' I treat them like every other human being, like they're smart and they're going to do great work. I'm sure some fall short, but I've got sixty-year-olds that don't do good work either. It's not like everybody for one hundred years was a fabulous worker and super motivated to concentrate."

Of course, he is correct; everyone is an individual. It's interesting to note, however, that many of Zingerman's business practices seem lifted from a book on appealing to millennials. For example, the company uses open book management, which offers employees complete transparency regarding finances, and makes everyone a stakeholder responsible for the financial health of the company. Additionally, the entire culture at the company stresses principles and beliefs, key intrinsic values of the millennial generation.

ZINGERMAN'S RECIPE FOR SUCCESS

Zingerman's is very prescriptive when it teaches its recipe for great service. But the company also encourages employees to be creative and adapt to situations as they perform each step of service, much like an experienced cook in an unfamiliar kitchen.

"Good cooks always adapt recipes to the setting," Ari explains. "The beauty of those steps is sometimes you're doing step three before you do step one because it's what's called for. It requires a creative application, just like a great cook adapts to the ingredients, adapts to the setting, adapts to the taste of a guest. But the recipe is still helpful for training new people to get them up to speed, and the better you get up to speed, the more you can be personal."

The two basic "recipes" that ensure consistency in the way service is delivered are below, but, as previously noted, employees can adapt as the situation requires.

Three Steps to Giving Great Service

1. Find out what the customer wants.
2. Get it for them accurately, politely, and enthusiastically.
3. Go the extra mile.

Five Steps to Effectively Handling a Complaint

1. Acknowledge the customer's complaint.
2. Sincerely apologize.
3. Take action to make things right.
4. Thank the customer.
5. Write it up.

These steps aren't just a means to improve Zingerman's bottom line (though they certainly help do that). Just like Nick Sarillo, who is profiled in Chapter Two, Ari and his colleagues believe that giving employees and customers outstanding service not only changes the workplace but also the greater community.

Or, as Ari puts it, "A lot of what energizes me around anarchist stuff is that it's really just about how you treat other people. So I think that when people adopt the mindset of giving great service everywhere, it goes better, and the world becomes better because you're treating everybody as an individual."

After talking with Ari, I'd say that in addition to Zingerman's overall recipe, he has one of his own:

1. Develop organizational principles and stick to them. At Zingerman's principles and beliefs are not just words on a web page. They are infused into the organization's DNA and every employee—from the newest sandwich maker to the managing partners—understands and implements them.
2. Treat everyone as an individual. Always.
3. Know your niche. Zingerman's hasn't tried to conquer the gluten-free market, but each Zingerman's business tries to be the best in its class.

CHAPTER 2

NICK'S PIZZA & PUB:
EMPLOYEES IN CHARGE

"I think what needs to happen as technology and artificial intelligence and all those things grow is that humans need to be more human, right? There's an opportunity there. That's when organizations realize that being more human is going to be their competitive advantage in the industry." **—NICK SARILLO**

A BRIEF HISTORY OF A NEW KIND OF PIZZA JOINT

Countless businesses across the United States were started out of a garage and many are still run out of one. Some of these ventures will only last months, while others may be sold for millions of dollars. Nick Sarillo, the owner of the Chicagoland pizza mini-chain Nick's Pizza & Pub, didn't start his first restaurant in his garage, however. When he couldn't find a family restaurant that catered to his entire family, kids and adults, he literally built it board by board from old barn wood.

Nick is a lapsed carpenter by trade, so he has the look of a guy accustomed to working with his hands, and he's fit, clean-shaven, and focused. Although he grew up working in his father's hot dog stand, which later morphed into a pizza place, he'd had enough of it by the time his high school graduation rolled around, and he decided to be a carpenter. But, after a few years working at McCormick Place, Chicago's premiere trade show venue, Nick got bored despite the hefty union paycheck. When a friend offered him a few side jobs in residential construction, he jumped at the opportunity. Then, as often happens, serendipity struck: his brother graduated from architecture school, and he and Nick decided to strike out on their own building houses. As time passed, Nick got married, started a family, and began building in Crystal Lake, Illinois, where he still lives.

It was at this point that he began to feel that the construction industry was increasingly prizing speed over craftsmanship, so he did a 180-degree turn and went back to the restaurant business. He saw a niche after noticing that if he and his wife wanted to take the kids out to dinner, they had to choose between a place where the food was good, but kids weren't welcome or the opposite—a place where the food was so-so, but all the bells and whistles made the kids happy.

"That's what gave me the idea to build this. It was really to have a place where kids could be treated as first-class citizens, like parents, and the family could come together and have a great time. And the neighbors could come together and have a great time. That's what initiated the business," he says, proudly.

So, Nick and his brother designed the restaurant, and Nick started building it from scratch on nights and weekends after he got home from his regular job. Little did he know that the old barn wood he was using to build the restaurant because it was so cheap would be all the rage today. Proudly showing off the wooden front door of the original Nick's in Crystal Lake, which has antique hinges that he built himself, he explains that his goal was to construct something that looked like it had been around for one hundred years so customers would immediately feel at home. And in 1995, that's exactly what he did. The result is a warm, homey space.

YOU'VE GOT TO HAVE BELIEFS

Like Ari Weinzweig, whom Nick considers "a brother from another mother," Nick credits the success of his ventures to aligning his beliefs with concrete actions. This didn't happen right away, however. "There's been a learning curve for sure," he says, smiling ruefully.

He recounts the early days, when he started implementing processes intuitively, "with a good heart and good passion" but not necessarily business smarts. "What I found is this process of systems I started implementing. Intuitively, I started with a lot of good things. I had a good heart and good passion, just wasn't all that smart." Nick credits Rudy Miick, a nationally known leadership consultant, with completely transforming his business and his life. He hired Miick in 2001 when he wanted to open more restaurants, but didn't want to "implode" like many others who got too big too fast.

"Rudy helped us define our purpose and our values. To me, that was a transformational part of my personal life too. I thought, 'This is how I've been searching for a way to create meaning at work.' I wanted to have work be something meaningful in people's lives. That's the key. That's the secret recipe. Those processes and all those things that I put in place, I became super focused on making sure that our purpose and values were alive and vibrant in the behaviors of our team."

Talking with Nick, I realized that pizza is only a means to an end, the vehicle the team uses to connect with one another and the community. Nick says maintaining the company's purpose and values are the foundation of everything. You can even see them for yourself on the company's website. Although they are somewhat reminiscent of

Zingerman's guiding principles, Nick's guidelines place more emphasis on *internal* relationships, which he believes lead to external success:

- We treat everyone with dignity and respect.
- We are dedicated to the learning, teaching, and ongoing development of one another.
- We have fun while we work!
- We provide a clean and safe environment for our guests and team members.
- We honor individual passions, and creativity at work and at home.
- We communicate openly, clearly, and honestly.
- We honor the relationships that connect our team, our guests, and community.
- We take pride in our commitment to provide quality service and a quality product.
- We celebrate and reward accomplishments and "A+" players.
- We support balance between home and work.
- Health: We are a profitable and fiscally responsible company. We support the physical and emotional well-being of our guests and team members.
- Our team works through support and cooperation.

For employees, these values are as important to internalize as the pizza recipe, which is also very specific: "The recipe of our sausage pizza is sixty pieces of sausage, nickel sized, finger-space apart, and has got to be done in sixty seconds. I mean, really six ounces of sauce. It's really, really specific."

According to Nick, there is a reason for the level of detail. It's not just about the sausage. "In order to get certified in orientation, you have to know our values. You don't have to memorize them word for word. You have to understand the behaviors behind them. We put a lot of intention into making them just as important as a recipe for our food."

That sounds nice, but if you're like me, you may be wondering how these values work in the real world, and if it's even possible to measure values and purpose. I was skeptical until he told me about numerous instances over the past several years when tips of over $1,000 have been given to servers in his restaurants.

"I'm a big fan of metrics and tracking data and measuring, whether it's financials or behaviors. I believe we can measure purpose, how it's showing up. To that point, our customers and our sales continue to grow. About a month or so ago, we had a server, Imelda, get a $2,500 tip. Servers getting over $1,000 tips has happened four or five different times in both restaurants, not just one restaurant. That's the data."

Remember, we're talking about local pizza restaurants in suburban Chicago, not fancy, three-star Michelin chophouses in New York or Paris.

To see how this could happen, let's go back and explore the ways the company's beliefs are put into action. It all starts with the job application, which lists the values of the organization on the first page and makes it very clear that applicants will need to buy into the system. The weeding out process starts there: 10 percent of the people hand the application back, explaining they're just looking for a job, not a new system of values or a new purpose.

COMMUNICATION IS KEY

Once someone has been hired, two equally important company values, communication and training, are emphasized. Nick's motto is "Trust and Track," a nod to the concept of "open book management," a management philosophy first articulated by John Case, a writer at *Inc.* magazine, and then promoted by Jack Stack of SRC Holdings in his book *The Great Game of Business: The Only Sensible Way to Run a Company.*

Employers who subscribe to this philosophy—a cohort that also includes Ari Weinzweig—believe in transparency, so they give employees a huge amount of responsibility not only over their own fate but also the entire company. They do this by teaching them how business "success" is measured before ensuring they understand the financials and other data critical to success. Employees, not managers, are responsible for improving their status and performance within the organization and have a direct "stake in the outcome," whether it turns out to be the company's success or failure.

Since communication is paramount in this style of management, Nick shows me the Communication Board, a place where employees write the "value of the day," things like being kind to others, along with the sales forecast for lunch and dinner. There is also a Results Board, which meticulously tracks cost, sales, and guest retention, and even how many people ask for specific servers.

This tracking is particularly important due to the way the profit sharing works. If you take a class (pizza making, for example) and are "certified" by your peer trainer, you are eligible for profit sharing. The more classes you're certified in, the more profit sharing you're eligible for. It's not a lot of money we're talking about here—when I visited, profit sharing totaled $7 per person for a period spanning the previous four weeks—but it can slowly add up. Plus, it changes the way employees think about the company.

"What's really cool are the conversations," says Nick. "One period it's $75 and the next period you get $7. They say, 'What happened?' I say "I don't know. You tell me what happened.' Now, we've created these ownership conversations."

Those "ownership conversations" lead to people working toward their own raises. The more certifications or levels they pass, the more money they earn. Managers don't decide when or what classes an employee takes; it's all up to the employee. Obviously, this type of system requires a significant amount of trust and transparency.

I can see the appeal of this approach and how this type of enthusiasm can be a self-perpetuating system. Nick is so persuasive and likeable that it's clear the people who work for and with him "buy in" to his approach 100 percent. Unlike Richard Coraine of Union Square Hospitality Group (one of the "Pragmatists" profiled later in the book), Nick doesn't think of his businesses as "cults." But his belief in what he espouses is rock solid and completely genuine. I don't know if this type of management could work for everyone, but it certainly works for him and his team.

This is illustrated by the passion with which he recounts his feelings when he realized his first restaurant was "going to make it." "You know, I think what all this comes down to for me is the first year I opened my restaurant, it was twenty hours a day, sleeping in the parking lot, getting up, coming in, and mopping the floors and that kind of stuff. Then I realized, 'Okay I'm going to make it. Now how do I build a big company?' That, to me, is what flipped the switch. I wanted people to enjoy coming to work every day. When someone walks out the door, I want them to say, 'You know what? That wasn't so bad. I'm looking forward to coming back tomorrow.' Because so much of our awake life is spent at work, why not have it be something meaningful and something you care about?"

MILLENNIALS: LEAD THE RIGHT WAY
AND THEY WILL FOLLOW

Like his "brother from another mother," Ari Weinzweig, Nick also disputes the notion that the millennial generation is different from the ones before it, arguing, "I don't think this generation is different from our generation. I mean, people are people. They're different and human. Everything is trainable. I believe people are good. Naturally they're all good inside."

The company motto, Trust and Track, allows his employees, many of whom are high school students and millennials, to steer their own destinies within the confines of work. For example, an employee can choose to stay in the same position for months, or receive more training and become an expert in it, or advance to a new position moving from expert pizza maker to salad beginner. It's up to them not their manager. This autonomy matches nicely with the ethos of the millennial generation. In fact, according to research by Espinoza and Ukleja—authors of the book *Managing the Millennials*, which I discussed earlier—the style of management at Nick's Pizza & Pub rewards many of the values millennials prize: self-expression, achievement, and, most importantly, meaning.

Unlike some people—okay, many people—Nick is incredibly upbeat about the millennial generation, believing they will initiate transformational change. "This generation is a great generation," he says. "They're going to make some great changes in our society. It just requires a different type of leadership, more authentic leadership. More transparent leadership. That's the nuance I think a lot of big organizations miss. They say 'Well, why aren't people engaged?'"

Nick says millennials need a purpose, as well as ways to demonstrate it within a measurable framework. That's why there's so much emphasis on communicating goals and measuring success, or as he calls it, "Trust and Track." Because employees understand the framework, they don't have to wonder about a yearly review or how they're doing. This approach cedes control to the workers and challenges them to solve their own problems within very specific boundaries.

"I'm not working to treat people with anything but respect. Then the other piece that I think really helps this generation is that we kind of get away from a control culture."

He goes on to explain that in a traditional company, when

employees have a problem, they go to their manager, who tells them what to do. Problem solved. Nick argues that if you do that, then the employees don't understand the values that were used to make that decision, so that's not how it works at his restaurants. If an employee of Nick's Pizza & Pub has an issue and approaches a manager, this is what happens: "We're going to walk over to one of the places that we have our values all over the walls. Maybe he doesn't have them memorized yet. I'd ask him, 'How would you solve the problem? Which value are you going to use to solve that problem?' By the way, the more values you integrate into solving the problem, the more effective the solution."

While this kind of problem solving may be preferred by the millennial generation, that's not necessarily true for baby boomers and gen Xers who grew up working in top-down organizations. But in the new model, leadership is just as accountable as everyone else. And, according to Nick, this is far from a bad thing:

"It's got to be reciprocal. If I can coach them, they can coach me. A lot of old guys are resistant to that. That's the difference in today's leadership. That's the expectation of this generation. They can't trust authority, right? Look what they've been brought up with. All the scandals. They can't trust the teacher or a politician, any of this stuff. The way I was brought up with authority, my boss told me what to do. I just did it. Nowadays, they're like, 'I want you to model. If you're telling me to do something, how are you doing it?' They have a different expectation of leadership. That's why it's got to be reciprocal for this work and for this generation, which is great."

Nick is a big believer in confronting issues when they happen. This makes sense, given that resolving conflicts offers another opportunity to put the company's values into action. "If we have a disagreement, instead of avoiding the conflict and saying, 'Let them cool off. Go work somewhere else and tomorrow will be better,' we say, 'We want you to actually step into the conflict and use these values to work through that conflict and come through the other side of it and feel safe.' That's how we create safe space. That's how we create trust. It's core."

It's clear that Nick's leadership style requires active engagement with employees, and he greeted each employee on a first-name basis as we walked through one of his restaurants. But, even though Nick provides first-person examples, it's equally clear that all his managers employ the same tools and tactics. In this way, his organization is not dependent on Nick to be the leader. According to Nick, the system actually works best when he is not required to be in the center of every decision.

TRAINING THE NEXT GENERATION THEIR WAY

As you might imagine, the training at Nick's is an intense process and one that's unique as far as I'm concerned. It starts with orientation, a two-day, ten-hour process centered around the company's values and culture. Then everyone, from full-time accountants to part-time hosts, goes into the kitchen for the next class, "101," and makes the most popular item on the menu, sausage pizza. After eating a piece of home-made pizza, they taste the other items on the menu, just like employees of Lettuce Entertain You, the iconic Chicago restaurant group that's the focus of Chapter Seven. Finally, after all that, employees break off into groups with their trainer for "201," which is job specific. In 201 they learn what they'll have to do and how they'll be held accountable.

Nick describes their training system as both an art and a science. "It's cool because again, we're going to put someone in side-by-side training for our first 201 class. Then we have a 1 to 5 scale. They have to get all 4's to be fully certified in their job. Then they're on their own. Now, if they want to, anything else they want to learn and do, their whole career development is right here. So many people on their first day of hire or in the interview ask, 'What's my career path like in this company? How do I move up in the company?' Here it is. It's right here on the wall. I think more companies could do that. After that first certification, anybody that wants to can become certified in another job. If a pizza maker wants to learn salads, they just sign up for Salads 201. They get a trainer and they train on salads one day instead of pizza making."

Many organizations have formal training procedures, but few allow the employee to take the initiative and move to a different position with more pay. At Nick's, after the first certification, an employee receives a 50-cent per-hour raise. And, after three certifications, the employee moves from "rookie" to "pro" and receives an additional raise. This pattern continues until the employee makes it to the "gold star expert" level. The key is that the career path for each employee is transparent and clear, and compensation is based on performance, not tenure.

As a result, it's not up to a manager to decide what an employee earns; it's up to the employee. Employees sign up for the next 201 class on a sheet posted in the back. If there isn't a class scheduled for a while, an employee can get one more person and then ask a trainer if he or she is available to teach the class, which can run anywhere from one hour to two days. Needless to say, that's not the way it works in a traditional restaurant or company.

This approach to giving direction to the millennial cohort has been validated by Espinoza and Ukleja. In *Managing the Millennials*, they write about the most effective ways to oversee younger members of the workforce. As the authors explain, "Millennials are super-like. Not unlike the man who wears the big red 'S' on his chest, they too have their kryptonite—it is called ambiguity. They hate ambiguity more than being micromanaged."[7] The authors continue that giving good

---

7   Chip Espinoza and Mick Ukleja, *Managing the Millennials: Discover the Core Competencies for Managing Today's Workforce* (Hoboken, NJ: John Wiley & Sons, 2016), 137.

direction to this age group requires "flipping *the attending to authority* bias to authority tending to employee development needs," which is probably the reason the training at Nick's fits the group so well.

Although Espinoza and Ukleja's research deal more with traditional managers, their findings undoubtedly apply to peer managers or trainers too. "The effective managers in our study shifted the focus from *perform for me* to *let's partner for performance*. It is important for manager and employee to find agreement about what is helpful to develop both parties' competencies. Partnering for performance requires that consideration and balance be given to the manager's goals, the millennial's goals, and the organization's goals," they write.[8]

It's uncanny how closely Nick's management and training philosophy reflect the desires of the millennial generation, at least as articulated (accurately, in my opinion) by Espinoza and Ukleja. I believe this is a big reason why his restaurants have been and continue to be so successful.

"Most of our team is above average because they've earned it themselves," Nick says. "It's not because a boss gave them a raise. We don't have to do reviews. Again, all that stuff is off the plate of a manager. The team is getting their own raises from rookie, pro, expert. There are different color hats that signify rookie, pro, and expert. Everybody knows what everybody else is making simply by looking at the chart on the wall or looking at what color hat they're wearing. It's pretty simple. If they want to be full-time, add a dollar to this, to whatever they're making, they get a dollar more."

It's not as if managers at Nick's have no role whatsoever. They're aware of what certifications people are getting because they're marked in the training folder everyone receives during orientation. It's up to the peer trainer, however, to certify them.

"At the end of every training shift, we have what we call a 'back

---

8   Ibid., 141–142.

loop.' Trainers pull the folders out and ask themselves, 'What's one thing you did well today? If you could replay the tape, how could you enhance your performance for both the trainer and the trainee?' Then on the other side, they get a 1 to 5 scale. They have to get all 4's before they get certified. If they want to move and do something other than what they were hired for, they have to get all 5's. They have to prove mastery in their job."

To show me a nuts and bolts example, Nick leads me over to the bar, where the bartender, Mike, is setting up for the day. To guide every task he's doing, Mike has an "ops" card, his own Trust and Track checklist that he has to follow. There's no manager checking his work, but Mike knows he must complete each and every item on the list. Tasks are so specific that in theory anyone could walk in the door and open the bar even if they'd never been there before. Once every item is completed, the ops card is flipped over as a signal to the other employees that Mike has completed his responsibilities and is accountable for his work.

Recently, Nick has begun teaching his Trust and Track system in a series of workshops with the goal of "inspiring leaders to influence transformation in their organizations by providing life-changing leadership education." The students range in age, occupation, and experience. Everyone who participates in the workshops—from the sixteen-year-old high school sophomore to the fifty-year-old business owner—has the same task: learn how to coach, handle conflict, and create a feeling of safety and accountability within an organization. Nick says it's all about experiential learning and emotional intelligence. If they complete the workshops successfully, they get certified, which means they can use the training at one of Nick's locations or at their own workplace, wherever it may be.

CULTURE: INTENTIONAL EXCELLENCE

All of this was fascinating to me, but I also wondered if the Trust and Track system could truly be replicated in other places. I ask Nick if the company culture was diluted when he opened his second restaurant and had less control.

"Actually, the opposite happens when we're really intentional about the culture and we define what we mean by excellence," he says. He then pauses and adds, "We define the culture that we want to have really clearly and then all the systems, support, and behaviors of that culture from top down, sideways, every which way actually influence the culture of the community that we're in."

As an example, he cites what happened when he opened his second restaurant in 2005. One hundred people were needed to staff it. In the first six months, they only lost four employees, an astounding retention rate considering a typical restaurant loses 50 percent of its staff in the first six months.

I ask him the reasons for this. Was it simply smart hiring or culture? He smiles and answers in one word: "purpose." He adds, "From a restaurant perspective, it's like, how do I bring this to more communities in America? You know, this kind of environment. This kind of community feel. All these families and neighbors coming together which is what I intended in the beginning. I think America needs more of that in our society."

When Nick and I spoke he was chomping at the bit to bring his leadership philosophy back to his hometown. Not long after, he opened a third restaurant in Chicago's busy Lincoln Square neighborhood, a part of the city already teeming with pizza restaurants and a world away from the sleepy suburbs. Speaking from personal experience, I know how difficult it is to instill a cohesive culture in a city as busy and complex as Chicago, but I'm betting Nick can do it.

NICK'S PIZZA & PUB'S RECIPE FOR SUCCESS

Nick Sarillo is a passionate leader. But he has learned, through trial and error, that passion alone does not create a great company culture. In fact, given the size of Nick's business, the level of detailed leadership tools the company uses is astounding. Nick's vision and values are as concretely inserted into the culture as the eight-foot wooden door at the front of the restaurant. And, in the end, Nick focuses on a few key elements.

1. The proof is in the details. Platitudes and praise are nice, but Nick has done the work to demonstrate to his employees that the company "says what it means and means what it says." You can see it in the Track and Trust structure, in the color-coded hats, and in the ops cards at each workstation

2. Strong leadership = accountability. Again, "accountability" sounds good, but it's meaningless unless managers walk the walk every single day. If accountability is baked into the culture, then the hourly employees understand the expectations and perform their tasks with enthusiasm and energy. That's how you can walk out of the restaurant with a $2,500 tip.

3. It cannot be stressed enough that Nick believes transparency, accountability, and authenticity are the keys to good leadership. Although these values were intuitive for him, research on millennials backs him up, demonstrating that those values motivate and inspire them.

4. Love what you do. You've got to believe in your vision. There is no room for lip service at Nick's Pizza & Pub. If you don't believe in the value proposition, Nick's is not the place for you. As a result, new employees are self-selecting, so embracing the company's vision is as fulfilling as one of the famous sausage pizzas.

CHAPTER 3

BERYLHEALTH:
EVERYONE DESERVES A "THANK YOU"

"I think that every employee at any company, in any industry, large or small, really wants three things. First, they want to feel like there is purpose beyond the job. Second, they want to feel appreciated for what they're doing. And third, they want to feel like there's the opportunity to learn and grow." **—PAUL SPIEGELMAN**

A BRIEF HISTORY OF BERYLHEALTH

Paul Spiegelman calls himself "an analog man in a digital world." And his success proves that when it comes to outstanding customer service, nothing beats old-school hospitality. He's got the type of personality that immediately puts you at ease. When we met to discuss his achievements at BerylHealth, a four hundred-person "concierge referral service" he built from the ground up, there was a turkey sandwich and chips waiting for me along with a cold bottle of water.

Paul says his obsession with hospitality started with his parents. He noticed that his dad never forgot a face—even one from decades before—and that people would come up to Paul and his brothers and tell them their dad was one of the nicest people they had ever met. Their sincere praise and admiration for his father stuck with him, and he has spent his working life trying to walk in his father's footsteps, he says. "I wanted to be somebody that people would talk about, not for what they did, but just for who they were."

A California native, Paul began his career as a lawyer, working alongside his father, but after a year and a half, he and his two brothers (he's the middle one) decided to fulfill a childhood dream to team up and run a business. Working together, they created a medical alert device to help frail elderly people who would need outside help if they fell.

In April of 1985, the three brothers took over one of the conference rooms in the law firm and created a device with a speaker phone that could be hooked up like a telephone answering machine and send an emergency signal. In the first of many strategically intuitive events, they decided to go to local hospitals and offer the service to patients who were being discharged with chronic, serious medical conditions.

From the beginning, Paul says, delivering good service came naturally, thanks to parents who raised three boys with good values, and who took to heart their father's advice to "be nice, never burn a bridge, and treat people with respect."

"People always ask me, 'When did you decide you wanted to do business this way?' The answer was, we never decided. It wasn't a business plan. We were going out to eighty-five, ninety-year-old people's homes and developing relationships with them. One of the customer service stories that comes to mind is an older woman who asked if we could get her some ice cream. She said she liked Häagen-Dazs butter pecan ice cream. So what did we do? We went to the store, got it, and brought it back for her."

What happened next is what often happens with start-ups: they had a lot of work and not a lot of income. They started by charging people $25 a month for 24/7 service, taking turns sleeping on a cot they dragged into the office. In the end, they were bringing in only $2,500 per month, barely scraping by and working nonstop. Nevertheless, they kept at it because they really believed in the concept. (They even tried to raise a million dollars in $15,000 dollar increments. Only one person, a friend of the family, invested any money.)

"So, we said, 'Let's just put our heads down, work hard, and hopefully good stuff will happen. Then, a series of events started that changed the course of what we were doing. It was a Saturday night, and I was working when a call came in. There was a ninety-three-year-old woman that had been beaten and stabbed, and locked in a closet. We ended up saving her life. Two days later, we get a front-page story in the *Los Angeles Times*. So, it didn't make us rich, but it kept the doors open. That was the first big thing."

SCALING UP

Once the ball got rolling, it didn't stop. Within the first year a hospital client asked Paul if he and his brothers would like to offer a physician referral service for people new to the area. Paul jumped at the chance and a new, much more profitable business was born.

"Two weeks later, we're answering the phone, 'Thank you for calling United Hills Hospital, how can we help you?' We had names of the doctors on 3″ by 5″ cards. Come to find out, every hospital in the country has this type of service, and most of them were doing it in-house. They had an eight-person staff doing it in bigger hospitals. That's really when our core business was born. We became an outsource provider of call center services to hospitals."

After two years, Paul and his brothers catapulted toward their dream by winning a contract to outsource referrals for a company with 350 hospitals across the country. Because they were going to build an additional call center from scratch, in addition to the one in Los Angeles, they looked around the country before settling on the Dallas-Fort Worth (DFW) area. With a $10 million budget and a lot of technical help from Paul's older brother, Mark, they set up shop in an old Walmart and BerylHealth was born. Although they lost the original client two years later, their company grew to service five hundred hospitals across the country. In just a few years, the brothers had transformed their early vision from a home health alert company to a fifty-person call center in LA to a four hundred-person "concierge referral service" called BerylHealth in DFW.

"We didn't just take all the calls and hook people up with hospital services. Our real value was that we tracked the demographics of the caller to determine whether they became patients at the hospital, and could tell the hospital, 'You spent this much on advertising (looking for new clients). Here's how many people became patients. Here's how much they spent. Here's the ROI, and this is why you should advertise more, and all of that.'" In this way, BerylHealth redefined the value of a call center operation.

Increasing the hospitals' ROI wasn't the only goal. The call center industry is notorious for high turnover and low morale, but Paul saw that by creating a strong internal culture where employees were engaged and valued, he not only retained employees but also clients. As the business grew, employees were also financially and personally rewarded, and the company benefited from employee and customer loyalty with increasing profits.

"You think of a call center, you think of low morale, boiler room operations, a low-margin business, high turnover. We said we don't want to be a business like that. We want to be a business that can create value, and we want to be able to charge a premium price for what we do. Well, that's hard to do in an industry where generally lowest price wins. It wasn't that far into our business—maybe we had en, twelve employees—and they would start to make comments to us, like, 'This is a really fun place to work,' and we said, 'Well what makes it fun?' They said, 'It seems like you guys genuinely care about us.'

"We were bewildered by that. Keep in mind, none of us had ever really worked anywhere substantial in our careers, but we were smart enough to realize that we had something there, and that if we created an environment in which our people really loved what they did, they were going to do a better job for us, and that was going to rub off on the customer."

The brothers no longer work as a team. Paul's younger brother died tragically of a brain tumor in 2005, and Mark left the business in 2000. At one point, Paul decided he wanted a partner, and in 2010 he agreed to sell BerylHealth to a private firm. Although he had signed a letter of intent to sell, he backed out, realizing the company's unique culture would not survive its new ownership. It was, he says, the "best decision I ever made."

SCALING UP—AND UP

One year later, a large, publicly traded medical waste disposal company, Stericycle, wanted to expand, and approached Paul to see if he wanted to sell BerylHealth but remain as CEO. Long story short, he said yes and sold the company in 2012—before realizing he wasn't interested in running his business within a larger company.

And that's when the CEO of Stericycle agreed to put him in a new position, chief cultural officer.

"I wanted to see if what we did in a small company could apply in a large company. I'd never worked in a big company so I wanted to see if it was possible to scale a big culture in a large public company. And, ultimately, could leaders change the way they lead, from a more command-and-control style to a much more collaborative, team focus?

I said, 'If you'll give me the opportunity to do that, I don't even want to be paid, because I'll be able to tell this story,' and the CEO said 'Let's start Monday.' So, basically, that's what I've been doing for the last five years."

By the time we spoke, Paul had transitioned out of his role at Stericycle, leaving the chief cultural officer position intact and in good hands. He is not gone from the business world, however, and is still very involved in the Small Giants Community, an organization focused on purpose-driven leaders, which he cofounded with author Bo Burlingham in 2009. (The term "small giants" was coined by Burlingham in his 2005 book, *Small Giants: Companies That Choose to Be Great Instead of Big*.) Small giants are value-driven companies and are often profiled in Paul's podcast, "Growing with Purpose." The entrepreneurs who lead them believe that a strong culture provides its own ROI, and if employees are engaged and treated well, the company will also be profitable. It's pretty much the opposite of a company whose only goal is meeting quarterly profits.

CULTURAL ROI

For Paul, as for so many leaders profiled in this book, hospitality—as defined by empathy plus action—must be applied internally and externally. This was the theme of his first book, *Why is Everyone Smiling? The Secret Behind Passion, Productivity, and Profit*, published in 2007. He wrote about BerylHealth's corporate culture and recounted specific instances of delivering "quality service" to internal stakeholders, from giving his car to an employee who walked to work to buying a plane ticket so another could visit his dying mother.

I find the story he tells about BerylHealth's first CFO, Pat, illustrative. When Pat came onboard in 2005, the company already had a committed, loyal workforce, and Paul saw a clear connection between employee engagement and customer loyalty—core components of the company's culture—and the financial success of the business. He wondered which of these components was the most important, while Pat wondered if the culture mattered at all.

"Pat came in and saw all the money we were spending on culture and events, and decorations, and all this kind of stuff. He was so cynical about that and said, 'Paul, I know the company's doing well, but I could really help impact our bottom line more if we got rid of some of that stuff.'"

"I said, 'Pat, I can't quantify this for you, but I've got to believe there's a connection between all of these.' Two years later, he had completely flipped. We were driving to see a customer in Indiana, and he said, 'Paul, you know, I've been thinking. It's kind of like a circle. If we get our employees to be loyal, that's going to drive customer loyalty. If those customers are loyal, that drives profitability. As a privately held company, we're committed to turn that profit back into our people, give them better tools and resources to do their jobs. The cycle simply continues.'"

And then, he expresses exactly what I said at the beginning of the book: that people are willing to pay a premium for outstanding customer service. "We were 30 percent more expensive than our next closest competitor. Why would anybody pay that much more for another company picking up the phone for their hospital? They paid because of our culture, because they knew that the environment would create a better experience for the moms calling in, and they were willing to pay more for that. That service mentality became our brand, and our brand is what really grew our business into being the leader, and ultimately was reflected not only in our pricing, but even in our valuation."

Once BerylHealth became part of the much larger Stericycle, Paul had to prove that fostering a positive culture did indeed offer a clear ROI. And he did.

"I used to present to the board every quarter, and I knew that I was going to have to show the ROI. I was able to show that our employee attrition had gone down. We measured it. In 2012, employee attrition had cost the company somewhere between $25 and $40 million dollars. And, that's just voluntary attrition. The next year, it went down by 5 percent. Well, that's $2 million dollars, directly to the bottom line."

"We were also able to show that our customer satisfaction scores were tracking exactly to our employee satisfaction scores, so they saw that relationship. Lastly, I remember looking at profitability by location. [Stericycle] had hundreds of locations in the US. Fifty percent of the most profitable locations were also the top ten most engaged. So happy people create happy customers and that creates more money." Of course, Paul had intuited this all along, but his new role forced him to quantify the benefits of happy employees. "I knew that I wouldn't have survived, nor would these efforts survive, if I couldn't go to this board and say this stuff matters."

THE CUSTOMER COMES SECOND

Countless organizations say that the customer is their number one priority, and some, such as Zingerman's and the Union Square Hospitality Group, truly mean it. Paul, however, has a different take, one that's well expressed in the title of his third book, coauthored by Britt Berrett and published in 2013. In *Patients Come Second: Leading Change by Changing the Way You Lead*, the focus is on hospitals, but the insights can apply to any organization.

Before I get into Paul's book, ask yourself the following question: "Would I rather have surgery at a hospital with engaged, happy employees or a hospital with dissatisfied, disengaged ones?" I think we'd all prefer the former, and that answer is exactly what Paul believes. In the description of his book he writes, "In any business, you can't take care of customers if you don't take care of employees. Healthcare is no different."

The book's premise is that hospitals must find ways to engage all their employees, from the nurses to the switchboard operators, so that they *want* to provide great service to their patients. Of course, patients are important, but he argues that there is a direct correlation between employee loyalty and customer loyalty. And, as the healthcare marketplace continues to face uncertainty, the pressure will continue to rise on patient acquisition and retention.

To Paul, happy employees lead to happy customers and, ultimately, more profit.

YOU'RE SPECIAL

Paul has always believed that employees want to feel appreciated and personally connected to the leadership, so as CEO of BerylHealth he introduced multiple systems to ensure that that happened. For example, in order to keep track of all his employees' life events—births, deaths, a child's graduation or wedding—he asked each manager to send him an email with the information.

"That would be my trigger to act. I could immediately write a personal note, visit someone in the hospital, make a phone call, whatever. We never missed anybody that way. So, we had this sort of backroom way of finding out what was going on in people's lives. And every month, I would write a handwritten note to everyone that had a work anniversary. I'd have the name of the person, how many years they'd been here, what department they were in, and then something about them personally that I might not otherwise know."

Grinning from ear to ear, he continues.

"Now, I have on my desk my note cards and I would say, 'Hey, Jane, congrats on seven years with Beryl. So great to hear that Jimmy won the softball championship this summer.' So, she gets this note at home from the CEO, and she's like, 'How did he know that?'"

"Did I honestly know everything that was going on? No. But, it got to me because we had a system, and then I was able to create a close relationship with every employee because of that. They all felt like the CEO knew and cared about them. That was one example of how we institutionalized a culture of caring."

Another way he kept communication lines open was to create an intranet site called "Ask Paul." The idea was that any employee could ask him a question and an answer would be published within twenty-four hours to the entire company. He imagined he'd get questions like, "What's the company's five-year plan?" or "Are we going to open another location?" That wasn't how it turned out.

"I got, 'Paul, when are you going to fix the toaster in the break room?' or 'The birds are pooping on our cars from the wires out in the parking lot. Can you fix that?' At first I thought, 'Wait a minute—I'm the CEO, why are you asking me that?' Then, I realized those things were important to them. What's important to them is important to me, and that's why I'm here. We gave people all these different ways to feel heard in the business."

EXTERNAL CUSTOMERS—TAKING CARE OF BUSINESS

Providing outstanding customer service—empathy and action—to internal employees (also called "internal customers") is the first step in the overall service process. The next step is giving outstanding service to external customers.

But how do you give outstanding customer service to a VP of marketing at a hospital a thousand miles away? One way was to get them to tour the facility so they would feel as appreciated as the employees.

"Before they even walked in the door, they get to their hotel, and they'd have a beautiful basket waiting for them, with a handwritten note card from me saying, 'Hey, we're so happy to have you here.' Our receptionist had business cards that said "Director of First Impressions," so they would see that right away. From the moment they came in they were treated specially. We had a photo booth in the back and we'd take a photo with them and send it home in a frame with them. Just all these little things that say, 'You're part of our family, too.'"

Coming from the restaurant industry, this kind of stuff seems like a no-brainer to me. Little extras like a piece of cake on someone's birthday or a free glass of wine to make up for poor service is pretty standard. What I don't understand is why more companies don't get that spending a little in the short run will pay off with increased ROI in the long run. Paul has wondered the same thing. He thinks the reason more companies don't "get it" comes down to leadership style and the current focus on quarterly profits at the expense of long term goals.

"The traditional command-and-control leadership style was really what created many, many successful businesses, and it worked for many years. Then, I think it just got to the point where financial pressures were so much that companies really had no choice but to keep doing what they were doing and are now very slow at making the change. I do believe and hope that moving away from command and control is the trend of the future. I still think we're early, but fifteen, twenty years from now, especially with millennials coming in, I think that it will be more of a standard way of doing business. This is the way business needs to be done."

BEST HIRING PRACTICES

I was curious about where Paul stood on the "nature vs. nurture" customer service debate. Does he think empathy can be taught, like Steve Hindy and Jerrod Melman (who are profiled in later chapters), or does he feel it has to be there from the beginning, like Richard Coraine (who is also profiled in a later chapter), Nick Sarillo, and Susan Salgado? It turns out he's pretty firmly in the "nature" camp, although he's also a strong proponent of building systems to keep employees—from the leadership team to the line employees—focused on service.

For Paul, it all goes back to his parents and the importance of applying the golden rule. In his opinion, teaching technical skills is easy; teaching emotional intelligence is not.

"We created an extremely robust hiring practice to do our best to try to get compassionate people, because we didn't feel like we could teach them that. We could teach them to use the computer and how to navigate the software. We could teach them the skills, but we couldn't teach them to have a heart."

"It takes a special person to do this job. In this case, they take eighty to ninety calls a day, six or seven minutes a call on average. How are they going to make that person calling in feel that compassion? The only way that we found that we could do that was to find people that came with compassion. I'd rather spend more time looking for that slice that gets it than feel like we're going to teach them how to do it."

He then launched into a story that demonstrated this point. It involved some of the sales managers he had met at Stericycle when he took on the role as chief cultural officer, including "Steve," an executive with more than one hundred disengaged, disenchanted employees who reported to him. Steve and people like him exemplify an all too common phenomenon in the corporate world, a phenomenon that led Paul to think, "What assholes—how did they get these promotions?"

He found that while the sales managers were hitting their financial targets, they were also making their direct reports miserable and causing high turnover. Thus, Paul set out to try to convert some of them, including Steve, a senior vice president with a terrible reputation. Since big companies are data-driven, Paul knew he had to use facts and statistics to prove the value of establishing a better culture.

"We started doing the employee engagement surveys [question-naires in which employees give feedback on various issues], which Stericycle hadn't done in years, and Steve saw the results. So, I approached him one day, and I said, 'Steve, I know last year, you had another great year, but it can't feel good when you read these comments of the people under you.'"

"He said, 'You're right, Paul. I actually felt really bad. I thought I was a good leader, but evidently, I'm not doing things the way I should.'"

"I said, 'Would you be open to the idea of simply [instituting] some subtle changes in style in the way you act, interact, and communicate every day? You'd not only continue to see the results, you'd get even better results. And you'd also get this warm and fuzzy feeling you've probably never had because you'd be having a positive impact on somebody's life and career.'"

Steve wanted to give it a try and began meeting with Paul on a regular basis. It started slowly. Paul first taught him how to talk to people in a new way and then encouraged him to become more engaged with the people around him. If his reports told him about bowling night, for example, he could stop by and give it a try. Slowly but surely, Steve began getting positive feedback from his reports, who couldn't believe he was the same person.

Unfortunately, Paul's "poster child" reverted to his old ways when the work became too intense and the demands seemed too insurmountable. He was ultimately fired—not because he didn't meet his financial goals, but because of the way he treated his colleagues, demonstrating that not everyone is capable of change, despite efforts to help them "get with the program."

MILLENNIALS: "I THINK YOU'RE TRYING TO BOIL THE OCEAN HERE"

When Paul talks about millennials, it sounds a lot like he's observed some of the same things as Lee Caraher, author of *Millennials & Management*, and Chip Espinoza and Mick Ukleja, authors of *Managing the Millennials.*

Like them, Paul has noticed millennials' confidence and the importance they place on finding a workplace that openly promotes values they find intrinsically rewarding. He also acknowledges some of the challenges in managing them, like their propensity to job hop.

"I've started to speak at local colleges and MBA programs, and I hear a lot of negatives like, 'Oh, those millennials. They jump ship every couple years. They've had this many jobs.' I look at it in a positive way. Good for them. I think that in general, they want something more than just a paycheck. They are, in general, looking to make the world a better place, have some impact on society, and more likely to rail against a command-and-control style leader. They're holding us accountable for being the kind of leaders that we all really should be."

Paul's desire to mentor people also fits nicely into the millennial worldview. As Caraher notes, millennials want and expect more access to senior management than previous generations. This access has resulted in what Paul jokingly refers to as his "millennial stalker," a young woman he's been mentoring who is brimming with confidence and chomping at the bit to make a difference.

"I'm already coaching her, [and] I've known her for a half an hour. I say, 'Whoa, whoa. Slow down. You know what? I think you're trying to boil the ocean here.' I tell her, 'This is all going to come. You've got plenty of time.' But I think I'm like an analog man in a digital world."

Being an analog man means continuing to write personal,

1andwritten notes and mailing them to people's homes. It means, Paul says, focusing on face-to-face interactions, not digital ones. It's not hat he naively thinks having a conversation will solve every problem. 3ut he does believe that emails and text messages are not an ideal vay to bring people together. For him, a lot of the old school rules, :specially the golden one, still apply.

"I still go back to looking for people who have an innate sense)f empathy and compassion and want to be in a place for the right easons. Then, I think it's upon us to give them purpose beyond the ob, appreciation for what they're doing, and opportunity to learn ind grow."

PAUL SPIEGELMAN'S RECIPE FOR SUCCESS

For Paul Spiegelman, like many others profiled in this book, there are several steps to ensure that a company's investment in its employees pays dividends with their customers and shareholders.

1. Take feedback seriously. If leaders ask for suggestions, they must deliver on them. Birds pooping on cars may seem beneath the job of CEO, but if it's a significant problem for employees, it should be as important to the CEO as any other issue.
2. Demonstrate a commitment to employees. Paul wrote notes, visited employees in the hospital, and showed he cared about them in multiple ways. This sincere concern for the people working for him engendered intense loyalty and helped BerylHealth achieve its financial success.
3. Use statistics to show the ROI of treating employees well. Paul proved that a decrease in employee attrition saved Stericycle $2 million in one year and that the company's customer satisfaction scores tracked exactly to its employees' satisfaction scores. He also demonstrated

through an internal survey that 50 percent of the company's most profitable locations were among the top ten locations with the most engaged employees.

Perhaps equally important to Paul's emphasis on his employees are his authenticity and consistency. The two qualities go hand in hand when you are talking about the kind of attention to detail that occurred on a daily basis at BerylHealth. As I never tire of saying, great leadership cannot be a slogan or memo—it has to be lived and exercised every day. You cannot expect to run a marathon without consistent practice, and running a company is no different. Moreover, employees, especially millennials, are not just looking for but expecting that kind of commitment from their leaders.

When I toured the BerylHealth call center with Paul, even though he had not been there in months due to his new responsibilities at Stericycle, one employee after another stopped to talk with him. At one point, he was cornered by a couple of excited people on a break telling him how their kids were doing and asking Paul about his family in turn. The magic was there, and it's no surprise that BerylHealth was ranked for several years as "One of the Best Places to Work" in multiple categories. The rankings came from *Modern Healthcare* magazine, the Society for Human Resource Management, and the Great Place to Work institute. Not bad for a call center!

THE TRANSFORMERS

Rob Siefker	**Mike McDerment**	**Steve Hindy**
(Zappos)	*(FreshBooks)*	*(Brooklyn Brewery)*

The three leaders profiled in this section have helped transform their industries. They recognize that change is inevitable and have helped ensure that their organizations evolve with the times. Not only do they acknowledge changes in workplace culture and their repercussions, but, equally important, they embrace it head on with purposeful direction. In the chapters that follow you'll read about a new management style called "holacracy," find out why sole proprietors don't have to stress about bookkeeping any longer, and learn how the craft beer movement started—among other fascinating lessons from the frontlines of American business.

CHAPTER 4

ZAPPOS:
IF YOU'RE NOT CHANGING, YOU'RE DYING

"You know, most companies are born and their destiny is to die, right? We want to build a company that lasts forever. And the only way to do that is to be more resilient and more adept at changing. And that's a big part of all of this. Most big businesses use their structure to keep it all together, to survive. But the structure can actually be your demise." —**ROB SIEFKER**

I'm going to start this chapter with a personal story about my wife, the COO of a Chicago-based tech company, and my two daughters, ages seventeen and twenty (I also have a thirteen-year-old son, but this story doesn't involve him). The night before flying to Italy for a family vacation, I walked into the living room and found my wife and daughters surrounded by a sea of shoeboxes and sandals. They were all frantically trying to find the perfect blend of fashion and comfort, the sandal that could stroll through the streets of Venice by day and stride confidently into a restaurant in Rome at night.

Since none of them had the time to look for shoes at a retail outlet, each had searched the website Zappos.com, placed a gigantic order, and hoped for the best, secure in the knowledge that the shoes would arrive the next day and they would have 365 days to return whatever they didn't want.

It's that kind of efficiency that people love most about the new economy. Moreover, Zappos, like FreshBooks in Toronto (discussed in the next chapter), has been recognized for its outstanding customer service ever since its founding in 1999. Now part of Amazon, which acquired the company in 2009 (for between $847 million and $1.2 billion, depending on the source), it has undergone seismic changes, from a small start-up with a traditional management style to its current system, which it calls a "holacracy." This system—described in greater detail a few pages on—replaces hierarchies and bosses with entrepreneurial "self-management." What fascinates me most about Zappos, though, is that through all the company's changes in scale and management style, its focus on delivering outstanding customer service is still a defining feature.

WHAT HAPPENED IN VEGAS . . .

On the surface, Zappos's Las Vegas headquarters looks like many other Silicon Valley tech companies, with ping pong tables and self-stylized workspaces. Yet, it's pretty clear from the moment you enter that the air is a little different at Zappos—and not just because it's 100 degrees outside the day I visit. There's an overarching sense of purpose.

Before sitting down with Rob Siefker, the senior director of customer service and director of the Customer Loyalty Team (the employees who work in the company's call center), I take a tour of the campus. It's housed in the old Las Vegas City Hall (a complex that included the city prison . . . yes, an example of a cell still remains). The company's move from the nearby city of Henderson was part of CEO Tony Hsieh's effort to revitalize downtown Las Vegas. As you might imagine, the company has a large footprint, but it feels intimate, with murals painted by current employees and a variety of collaborative work areas. In many ways, Zappos is the market leader when it comes to employee engagement, and in turn, customer service delivery. It's a place where the spirit of enthusiasm and genuine workplace harmony truly seem omnipresent. Case in point: call center employees are commended, not criticized, for how long they stay on a call to solve a customer dilemma.

ABOUT ROB SIEFKER

To understand how Zappos evolved into a holacracy where employees are expected to self-direct and self-manage, you have to go back to the company's early days.

And there is no better person to guide us through these early days than Rob, who started his career at Zappos as a temp in 2004. Accordingly, he has had a bird's eye view of the tremendous amount of changes that have occurred over the years. And there have been a lot. It's not hyperbole to say that Zappos is in the midst of an ongoing experiment in which it's both the researcher and the subject. In 2016, business writer Jennifer Reingold chronicled some of the aspects of this extreme makeover in an outstanding and informative article for *Fortune*. The article's title seemed to express the promise and the perils of the experiment: "How a Radical Shift Left Zappos Reeling."

But first, back to Rob's story. As a temp he was a part of the Customer Loyalty Team and he worked alongside about thirty other people in the Bay Area, the location of the original Zappos site before its corporate move to Henderson, Nevada and, ultimately, Las Vegas. His "training" back in the Bay Area consisted of spending three hours on the Zappos website on his first day, and then sitting with and observing someone on the phone for the next two days. Once he started taking calls, there was no feedback process and no specific mandate other than to "wow the customer."

Rob recalls being skeptical the company would even survive. "I started in college in the Bay Area in 1998, and I graduated in 2002. I had seen so many companies go out of business with the boom and the bust of the dot-com, Silicon Valley situation. My first impression was, 'Here's another dot-com company that's doing something crazy and they think they're going to be able to be successful and they won't be.' That was my first impression."

The company did survive, however, and Rob, now a seasoned employee who had been promoted to the team handling more complex customer service issues, moved with Zappos from the cocoon of Silicon Valley to Henderson, Nevada, in June 2004.

ORGANIC, FREE-RANGE GROWTH

You may not work in the tech industry, but if you've ever watched the television show *Silicon Valley* or seen the movie *The Social Network*, you know that growth within the industry can be explosive and chaotic, both exhausting and exhilarating. After the move to Nevada, Zappos had to start hiring very quickly. But to do this successfully, they needed a formal training system in place.

The main issue was how to hire a slew of new people while preserving a culture that was truly customer obsessed and a lot of fun. Reingold described the company's culture as a "quirky mix of circus, therapy session, and revival meeting." (She meant this as a compliment.) The aforementioned quirks, she wrote, "[exemplify] what has made working at Zappos so special: an obsessive focus on creating a culture that embraces the idiosyncrasies of each individual."[9] Reingold's description of "quirky" certainly matches my experience in the Las

---

9   Jennifer Reingold, "How a Radical Shift Left Zappos Reeling," *Fortune.com*.
    https://fortune.com/zappos-tony-hsieh-holacracy/ (accessed June 20, 2017).

Vegas office, where work stations are extravagantly decorated to reflect individual personalities. Zappos creates a genuinely fun environment where employees seem comfortable and at ease. Employee artists decorate the walls throughout the complex, and, at least during my tour, groups were meeting in formal and informal settings to discuss daily challenges and tasks.

Old-timers like Rob completely bought into the idea that great customer service could drive the business forward, and even make a difference in the wider world, by changing the perception of working at Zappos. The question was how to convey that mission and passion to people who just wanted a paycheck. Although "wowing the customer" was embedded into the DNA of the company, Zappos had no formal, written company values or processes in place to realize its mission.

It was, Rob says, a very challenging period for the people working in the call center, a.k.a. the Customer Loyalty Team.

"We were desperate to hire. We didn't have internal recruiting, and we didn't know how to frame the questions we wanted to ask candidates. We just wanted to put butts in seats, so to speak. And that's not a good place to be for any business, especially when you're talking about customer service."

In fact, the company's growth was so explosive that it became almost too much to handle. As Rob recalls, during the holiday season in December 2004, he would walk into work and there would already be fifty to sixty customers in the queue waiting more than ten minutes to talk to someone on the phone. This was not the way to "wow" anyone.

"We knew we weren't doing a particularly great job, but we were just growing so fast. We had our first million-dollar day in sales that November, and that was a big moment for us. So, it was still exciting, but we just didn't know how to hire appropriately. There are so many things going on when a company's growing so fast. We were just hanging on."

Unlike some of the other companies whose leaders I spoke with for this book, Zappos grew so quickly that its structure and formal recognition of its values seemed to spring from necessity, not from a vision or plan. Rob agrees with this assessment, adding that imposing structure was a way to rein in the chaos that followed the explosive growth in personnel and sales.

"We had no systems in place. We didn't have time to develop them. We were literally just trying to make sure we continued to run the operation. We were barely figuring out how to hire people, let alone how to develop them into different types of roles and identify what skills were needed. We were literally building the infrastructure of the place and then trying to figure out how to do a better job. We still knew we had to provide great service. That was *always* part of it, but we just learned as we went."

Looking back on it now, Rob can see how "being the darling of the internet" not only affected the company's bottom line (gross sales increased from $70 million to $1 billion between 2003 and 2008 (Tony Hsieh, *Harvard Business Review*, July/August 2010), but also how employees saw themselves within the company—especially after Zappos established its "ten core values" in 2006. (More on those later in this chapter.)

"I think that the growth (in the mid-2000s) contributed to that buy-in and the rallying around the success of the business, our culture, and core values. We were unique and different. We wanted to change the way the world thought about customer service and that growth cycle impacted the heart of our attitude and mindset of the business. It was a very exciting time for us."

GROWING PAINS

About ten to fifteen years ago, Zappos's management structure was still traditional. Though managers were very responsive to employees' concerns, solving problems, running teams, and making changes in policy were tasks that fell under their authority alone. As Zappos continued to grow, it was recognized by *Fortune* as one of the top 100 Best Places to Work for six years in a row, from 2008 to 2014. The idea that outstanding customer service should be given while simultaneously "creating fun and a little weirdness" (core value number 3) seemed to be working well.

However, that style of management was slowly and deliberately being phased out as CEO Tony Hsieh decided that the company would begin to transform into a holacracy. This innovative business model was developed by Brian Robertson, an independent former programmer with little management experience. The philosophy theorized that the power struggles endemic in traditional business hierarchies do not allow companies to reach their full potential. These challenges limit human potential and, ultimately, a company's growth potential.

Following conversations with Robertson, Hsieh was convinced. In the new "bossless" organization that Zappos has become, myriad work circles replace top-down reporting lines. Employees have roles within the circles, not specific job titles. People called "lead links" (or, in other organizations, managers) can encourage employees to take on certain responsibilities, but they cannot force them to do something they don't want to do. For example, unlike in a typical "top down" system, if a lead link asks a member of the Customer Loyalty Team to work extra hours, the employee is not compelled to accept the responsibility. That said, the hope is that employees embrace the Zappos Family Values and, as a result, help support the organization as a whole.

The transition to this completely different system was rocky. In March 2015, Hsieh sent out an unusually firm email basically saying that if you couldn't get with the program of self-management, the company would pay you to leave. It was a huge jolt to the employees, especially because only about half the company was fully participating in the holacracy system at that time; the other half was slowly dipping their toes into the water.

For its part, the leadership team didn't expect the ensuing turmoil.

In retrospect, Rob believes that the email was misinterpreted and that the huge changes in the company's structure should have been implemented differently. It wasn't that leadership didn't matter or that employees could do "whatever the hell they wanted," the idea was that you could do whatever you wanted as long as it truly drove the business forward (that is, served the purpose of the organization and its customers). Unfortunately, as veteran managers left, things became chaotic, and the company was left with a lot of inexperienced employees who didn't understand the culture or direction of the company.

According to Reingold, Zappos experienced 29 percent turnover in 2015. Moreover, she writes, "The result has been an epic clash between a doctrinaire set of rules and a culture whose very essence has been a tolerance for the unruliness that comes with individual self-expression."[10] Nonetheless, Zappos stuck to its core values.

"It was a hard time for me because I saw the leaders on my team just go to the sidelines because it was so stressful," says Rob. "People were not in a good place at that time. It was tumultuous and confusing for everyone in the organization."

"I don't know if we realized how challenging [the transition] was going to be for our employees. We always had this very strong culture and we were radically transforming it, stripping away what people knew about how to run the business in terms of the structure and how authority was distributed. I think we underestimated how challenging that was going to be for us."

---

10 Ibid.

It was a challenging time, but the company's leadership, especially Hsieh, believed that the transition to holacracy was critical to the long-term success and growth of the organization, while maintaining its entrepreneurial spirit. Some employees thrived in the new entrepreneurial culture, but many didn't. Rob and others realized they had to hire people with certain traits, characteristics, and personalities, and purposefully help everyone evolve into their new roles.

"We still have people that are predominately doing customer service jobs, but we also want to have people that are able to problem solve, both on behalf of the customer, but also on behalf of the company. And, we have to hire the right people because sometimes the environment is very challenging. One, customer service is not easy on a day-to-day basis. But handling the changing environment of Zappos is also challenging, and you have both of those components. Some people are built better for it than others."

To help new hires adjust, Zappos instituted an onboarding system to explain holacracy to them. The idea that employees "controlled their own destiny" needed context and a lot of explanation; an employee shouldn't wind up deciding that because they have control over their time, working at a swimming pool three days a week was okay. The company had to carefully teach them about its culture of hard work and core values. The whole idea, Rob says, is to get back to the culture he found when he stepped through the doors in 2004. "We want to bring back more of that entrepreneurial culture where employees own their part of the work and then just go after it, not because someone's telling them they should. If there's a problem, we want them to solve it on their own. We used to do that. Now it's a bigger company and I think trying to be able to replicate the ability for people to do that is what this is all about, having that more entrepreneurial spirit around each group and area of the business that people can feel that they can impact."

The way he sees it, as the company grew, some employees, especially in the call center, weren't given the tools to problem solve and weren't asked to make decisions on their own. The goal now is to give them a pathway to learn or relearn how to do that, and the hope is that this will fundamentally change the organization so that it's more resilient and able to handle whatever the future brings. By getting away from a traditional hierarchy, the company hopes that everyone will be more invested in its success and have the tools to make a positive impact, whether that's in their own small circle or throughout the organization at large.

There have been some ups and downs, especially in the call center—the "eye" of the customer service experience. Here, Rob's team has focused on developing Zapponians (the term coined to describe Zappos employees) who will advocate for customers in this new environment. What they realize now is that without coaching, direction, and mentoring, it's easy to lose a sense of purpose and descend into chaos. It's been a challenging journey and has taken time to refine the overall message: Employees can pursue their individual goals and make an impact, but they still have tasks they're accountable for within the new structure.

I asked him if the whole "wow the customer" idea he found when he started working at the company still exists after the transition to holacracy. As far as my wife and daughters are concerned, Zappos still offers fantastic service in the form of efficiency as well as friendly, enthusiastic call center representatives.

"We're a different business than we were in 2007, and I think that's a good thing. I think we've gotten infinitely better. I look back, it's night and day where we were in 2015 to where we are today. The hyper tumultuous period, the ripping the Band-Aid off and saying, 'Hey, everybody, we're going to do it differently,' that is over. A great brand is a story that never ends. We're all there now, but we're on different pages of the story. We're not yet on the same page. It's still the same story and same dream that we're trying to live. From the moment that someone's hired, they know that we're all about customer service. If they don't see that they're not paying attention."

ZAPPOS FAMILY VALUES

Like many of the organizations profiled in this book, Zappos now has formally written core values, reflecting their internal culture and promoted throughout the organization.

The Zappos Family Core Values:

1. Deliver WOW Through Service
2. Embrace and Drive Change
3. Create Fun and A Little Weirdness
4. Be Adventurous, Creative, and Open-Minded
5. Pursue Growth and Learning
6. Build Open and Honest Relationships with Communication
7. Build a Positive Team and Family Spirit
8. Do More with Less
9. Be Passionate and Determined
10. Be Humble

Though it's had a strong customer service culture from day one, Zappos didn't establish formal, written core values until 2006, seven years after it was founded. By then the company already had hundreds of employees and was known for its quirky culture, so I wanted to know how they came up with the ten values.

Like a lot of things at Zappos, it seems the values grew organically as employees at every level of the organization tried to define the qualities and attributes of the culture and the very best employees (or "Zapponians"). Management sought employee input, believing that if employees shared ownership in the decision they would more readily buy into the culture. As a result, the values weren't dictates from above but a semi-democratic decision. Thus, from an original list of thirty-seven core values, employees helped whittle down the list to the ten they still have today. The finalized list was a huge relief for Rob as it gave him more clarity in how to hire and make decisions.

"I thought it brought the right kind of mindset regarding how we wanted to look at things. I've always said our core values are kind of our compass. Not every decision is going to be easily decided upon. Sometimes you have to make tough decisions, but you use the framework of the core values to give you some guidance. They also gave us an idea of who we wanted to hire and the skills we were looking for. We wanted individuals that exhibited these core values naturally."

And, it's not as though Zappos is a free-wheeling commune where Zapponians are without structure. In some ways, as I experienced it, daily operations are similar to those of other organizations I have visited, but with the added sense of personal investment throughout all aspects of the process. Typical meetings might include more employee "sharing" around non-work specific activities, but then it's down to business. At its best, all employees feel empowered to share their views as part of the creative process.

Zappos is now owned by Amazon, the world's third-largest retailer, which as far as I know has never been described as having a Zappos culture. In fact, one point of pride at Zappos is that Amazon has never asked or expected the culture to change or conform to the larger Amazon model.

As the company has grown, the ways in which its culture is preserved have altered. It's no longer practical, for example, to send out surveys and get feedback on Zappos culture from employees as often as they once did. But there are now people whose job entails devising ways to maintain a culture of intimacy and stay true to Zappos's core values even though the company now numbers more than twelve hundred people.

Preserving that culture also depends on careful hiring. In Rob's opinion, you can teach people to answer the phone but you can't teach them how to be "an amazing person." Consequently, he believes that the holacracy culture at Zappos is painful for people who don't have empathy, the capacity for change, and the ability to work well within a team. Employees with bad attitudes aren't tolerated. It's everyone's responsibility to work toward making the company the best it can be.

MILLENNIALS—THEY'RE JUST LIKE US!

As I'm speaking to Rob, I realize Zappos has met head on both the challenges and opportunities posed by the millennial generation, and survived to tell the tale. The core values and attributes the company prizes are also ones that are particularly in tune with this generation. As many have written, millennials are positive, energetic, determined, and passionate. They want to have fun while at the same time make real contributions to society and the organizations they work for. They want to challenge the status quo and don't believe in hierarchies.

On the flip side, I think much of the turmoil Zappos experienced could have been avoided if they had recognized that their employees, especially the millennials who make up the majority of the staff, needed clear guidelines and direction to implement the changes in the company's structure.

Rob agrees with me about this. He then shares a few personal experiences that could have been taken straight out of a generic "How to Manage Millennials" book.

"I'll give an example. I posted a position that I needed to hire for internally and I had somebody who had been at the company for five weeks apply for it. And he showed up to the interview and had no idea what the position was or why it was needed. No context. We would have people coming into the call center who thought they could go do something completely different the moment that they got hired. We'd say, 'Well, no, we need people to answer the phones, that's why we hired you.'"

In these employees' minds, they had signed on to pursue their dreams; this was possible to an extent, but they didn't understand their role within the company, or the context of the company's values, because no one had explained them properly.

"Amazingly, it's not always obvious to people. You have to paint the right picture for them and give them the right mindset for them to be successful and then create that dream for themselves. Without that, they're kind of lost."

After these kinds of experiences, Rob realized he had to change the entire hiring and onboarding process, especially for those at the call center, where turnover is higher than in other departments.

"Now we're hiring people that are a better fit because we understand what qualities are needed to help people excel. The second part of that is the leadership development side of it. People need to have good coaches and mentors that can help direct them and keep them moving in the right direction . . . so that they can contribute and learn and become resilient, high-performing Zapponians."

To help them reach this goal, Zappos now has an "incubation" period for its call center employees, a two-month onboarding process that includes four weeks of "standard training" and an additional three to four weeks in a semi-controlled environment where they aren't just learning a specific job but also being further "molded and trained" to succeed within the Zappos culture.

Walking around Zappos, I felt like a grandfather amidst a sea of fresh faced hipsters. It's not far from the truth, considering the oldest person on Rob's leadership team is forty-one. But I wasn't surprised there were so many young people. Zappos has all the perks of a tech company along with the cool vibe and great press that go along with it. Accordingly, I admit to being a bit surprised when he told me there are people a few years shy of retirement working at the call center; apparently they also enjoy the fast pace and have the same energy and attitude that their much younger colleagues have.

That's why Rob doesn't necessarily associate the characteristics of a good "Zapponian" only with millennials, though he concedes millennials have been shaped by different expectations about the business environment.

"There are certain mindsets and characteristics that are more prevalent in certain individuals. Maybe that's more likely in younger groups just based on the world that they're growing up in. Anybody that's older and worked in the '70s, '80s, and '90s probably didn't ever dream that there were going to be these kinds of possibilities in the workplace."

The radical move to self-management may indeed be the wave of the future due to a number of congruent forces—millennials' expectations, fewer full-time jobs, and globalization, to name just a few. If so, then Hsieh and the Zappos team will have been right to swim out to the wave and ride it early despite the bad breaks along the way.

ZAPPOS'S RECIPE FOR SUCCESS

It's clear that Zappos is not the type of organization to rest on its laurels. In fact, much of its success lies with the company's ability to recognize innovative methods and tackle them head on. Ultimately, this has allowed Zappos to re-envision its customer service model and look at how to provide every employee with a roadmap for delivering exceptional service to consumers. Here's what the rest of us can learn from their hard-won experience:

1. Invest in your employees. Even if you think some of the Zappos holacracy ideas are too far out there for your organization, it's clear that genuinely engaging with employees has long-term positive effects on how employees view themselves and their company.

2. Along those same lines, encourage employees to be part of the process. Zappos is an example of the benefits of investing employees in a company's outcomes.

3. If you establish a set of company values or core principals, they should really mean something to everybody in the organization and be referenced on an ongoing basis—not just be on a plaque in a corner office. And, again, a great organization like Zappos includes employees in the process.

4. Especially in the context of today's millennial employees and the generation following them, organizations need to be nimble enough to adapt as expectations change. The "my way or the highway" management style has run its course. Moreover, this shift should be seen as an opportunity rather than an impediment.

5. Zappos has built a brand on the recognition that excellent customer service delivery starts with nurturing employees. This means that each member of its team not only understands the company's goals, but also has the tools and support to achieve them beyond expectations. This, in turn, has lasting benefits for everybody who comes in contact with the organization—and significant financial benefits for the company itself.

Sometimes in today's economy we associate quality service with speed. There is some truth to this idea; personally, I love being able to go online, easily navigate through a website, and place my order in a matter of minutes. Plus, when the right product arrives at my doorstep the next day—or even the same day, in some cases—I marvel at the "great" service experience.

That said, I also acknowledge that human interaction is important. Humans are communal. Those organizations that can differentiate themselves to their customers by making one-on-one connections even in the face of the internet's incredible efficiency are likely to find long-term success. In Zappos's case, the decision to empower employees and nurture successful human interactions demonstrates that this can be done—and done well. More importantly, it teaches us a lesson about how remaining true to one's core values and vision is a means to a better, more profitable end.

CHAPTER 5

FRESHBOOKS:
IT'S ALL ABOUT THE ROCK STARS—A.K.A.
CUSTOMER SERVICE

Mike McDerment: "The culture is way bigger than me. It's not a cult of Mike here."

Dan Sachs: "Well it started out that way, more or less."

Mike McDerment: "I don't think [of it] as a cult of Mike. I think [of it as] a cult of, 'I want to be in a company that helps people and actually is dedicated to customers, a company that works really hard at building great products.' Those things aren't Mike per se."

If you're a sole proprietor or the owner of a small business, you know that one of the most challenging things is staying on top of the financials when all you want to do is deliver your service or manufacture your product. Mike McDerment, cofounder and CEO of FreshBooks, a cloud-based accounting software company in Toronto, Canada, knows *exactly* how you feel.

In 2003, Mike was the head of a four-person website design business that he had dropped out of business school to start. One day, he accidentally saved over an old invoice. Instead of cursing his own stupidity and then moving on like most people, he decided to do something about it. He spent the next two weeks coding a computer program that would be more user friendly than Microsoft Excel. By the end of that time, he had laid the foundation of what has evolved into FreshBooks, a three hundred-person company whose mission is to "reshape the world to suit the needs of self-employed professionals."

GROWTH CANADIAN STYLE:
FREE RANGE AND SUSTAINABLE

FreshBooks started out in Mike's parents' basement in Toronto less than fifteen years ago. In 2016 it was not only recognized as "The Best Workplace in Canada" (for a medium-sized company) by the Great Place to Work institute but also as a company "that keeps its millennials from quitting"[11] by cnbc.com. To learn how Mike kept all of these millennials around (and other things), I caught up with Mike—and his dog—at the FreshBooks headquarters.

The office is located in a relatively quiet neighborhood, and it shares its building with a self-storage company. It took me a while to find the entrance, but then I was able to circle around to the back and take the elevator up, where I then walked into an innovative, open, and very "techy" looking office space. Mike's office—maybe 8 x 8 ft.—is a glass-enclosed conference room off the main workspace, which is open. Mike himself is about 6'5" and is wearing shorts and a T-shirt. When I arrive, I catch him running back and forth from one work group to another until we finally catch each other's eye.

Before we start chatting, he gives me a quick tour that includes a stop at the company kitchen/cafeteria for a glass of water. It's a very

11 Catherine Clifford, "How One Company Keeps Millennial Employees from Quitting," https://www.cnbc.com/2016/09/19/how-one-company-keeps-millennial-employees-from-quitting.html.

comfortable environment, and I feel at ease immediately as I observe various teams collaborating in the kitchen and at work stations. We settle into Mike's office, which is purposefully located near the bathrooms to encourage employees to stop by and chat.

I was there to find out how FreshBooks developed such a strong culture of customer service along with a mission and workplace that appeals to millennials. One of the things that I found so interesting about FreshBooks was that, unlike some of the other companies that I've visited over the years, FreshBooks developed a culture of outstanding customer service organically without ever talking about it. This may have something to do with the fact that the last job Mike had before owning his own website design business was leading canoe trips at a camp. (Perhaps catering to an audience of tweens and teens provided good experience for his current line of work.) Regardless, Mike feels that the lack of a roadmap was ultimately a benefit despite the bumps along the way.

"People tell me, 'Hey, other companies don't do this. It's not software culture,'" he says. "I didn't know that. It's made some things take longer than they needed to, but I think a lot of the things that make this place special and different are because when you go and learn something somewhere else, you start doing stuff and don't necessarily think about *why*. There were parts of our growth story that could have been less painful or happened faster. But then I don't think you get the magic."

When Mike started FreshBooks, he was still trying to run the website design company he'd developed. Facing the fact that it was too tough to do both, he transitioned out of the latter to focus on the company that's here today. Along the way, he had to learn everything from scratch, from building the company's software and marketing it, to scaling his services, all the while fighting to retain clients and employees.

"We were really obsessed with customer service from the get-go. We were very concerned with our quality. We were very timely with our responses, always answered the phones. We put our phone number on our website from the earliest of days, even when we were trying to make our company look way bigger than we were. We staffed over the holidays. We were always on for customers."

FreshBooks's passion for focusing on and rewarding outstanding customer service is built into the DNA of the company and comes from Mike himself—a guy who readily concedes there are people who don't find him empathetic upon first meeting him. However, he adds, "I'm unusually good at putting myself in other people's shoes. I'm not perfect, nobody is. I don't always get it right. But when I'm talking to a client, I transition into, 'What problem are you trying to solve? How can I help you do that?' I'm wide open at those times."

Although I'm in my fifties now, I still can totally relate to his missteps. It's hard starting a business when you're in your twenties because it's more expensive, time-consuming, and challenging than you can ever imagine. That's one of the main reasons why so many new businesses fail even if they start out with a great idea. Mike isn't afraid to talk about the times he almost failed, and he's justifiably proud of making it through to the other side.

He says the company hit a wall at eighty people; there was so much to do and so much to organize that no one even knew what the mission of the company was. That's when he decided the entire organization needed a day to come up with a mission statement. It began with teams each going to four consecutive "stations" that would help them brainstorm. One, for example, featured a video of the author and motivational speaker Simon Sinek giving a TED Talk titled "How Great Leaders Inspire Action" (one of my personal favorites). It's based on Sinek's 2009 best-seller, *Start with Why: How Great Leaders Inspire Everyone to Take Action.*

It all seemed like such a good idea at the time, but good intentions don't always lead to good outcomes. "The day did not go like I'd hoped it would," says Mike. "Very well-intentioned, but a failure. We did not get a mission statement out of that thing. I left that day, and I thought the sky was falling for six or eight weeks."

But the sky didn't fall. Instead, Mike hired a COO who had experience operating a large company. The next series of company-wide meetings included specific steps to help employees take action to solve all the day-to-day issues. But, in the end, FreshBooks still lacked a mission statement. This missing piece was always in the back of Mike's mind until a few years later, when he thought more about his own experiences as a small business owner and the people he knew who were also self-employed, either by choice or necessity.

"Our insight is the world is not built for self-employed professionals or their teams, which is not surprising because we grew up in the age of corporations. Then you start to look at how the world [is] set up for [self-employed] people and the short answer is not well at all. That's where we come in."

Thus, the company's mission was born: "To reshape the world to suit the needs of self-employed professionals and their teams." And it has had a profound influence on the company's culture.

FreshBooks is at the right place at the right time. According to the US Bureau of Labor Statistics, 10.1 percent of the US population was self-employed in 2016, and that number is expected to grow significantly over the next decade.

CULTURE: FRESHBOOKS'S SPECIAL SAUCE

Now that the company has more than one hundred employees, Mike is delighted to have a strong leadership team that he can rely on to focus on some of the areas he isn't as interested in. As he says, business is a "team sport." And like other leaders profiled in this book, Mike is emphatic that company culture all comes down to the people that you hire and how you treat them.

"When I started, we called the people in customer service 'Rock Stars.' You'd be doing support three days a week and had two days to do other stuff, which was generally around serving customers in one way or another anyway. So the folks we hired were the kinds of people on a mission to serve people and customers."

Like so many of the leaders I spoke with, FreshBooks intentionally hires people who find meaning in serving others. I'm convinced this helps build a cohesive culture.

"That's at the heart of what we want to understand when we interview you. Do you derive satisfaction from serving others? Are you intrinsically motivated to help people? Do we believe you could be good at it because you're motivated? It's hard to teach that. Then it becomes this flywheel where everybody is like that."

He continues by describing an example of how empathy was put into action—the definition of hospitality. One day, a visually impaired customer tried to get in touch with the company over the internet. As a solution, FreshBooks sent him a "crazy contraption" that he could use to direct his mouse. To Mike, "solving that kind of problem is the result of a carefully crafted culture that recognizes and rewards that type of behavior [even though] we're a tech company, not a restaurant or hotel."

Of course, he also admits that there have been times his team has taken the internal message of doing anything to help a customer a bit far.

"We've had instances where people would say, 'I'm sorry that happened to you—I'm going to refund the last three years of your account.' My thing there would be, 'Okay, that is probably not in line with what was necessary to do here. That's probably too far. Let's try and learn from that. The person was trying to do the right thing for the customer, and that's great, but we can't give away three years of somebody's account every time something goes wrong."

I can relate. I remember many years ago wanting to take care of a very good customer in my restaurant, Spruce. The guest arrived entertaining a party of seven other executives for a special dinner with a full tasting menu and expensive wine—the works. As the entrees were served, one of the orders was incorrectly prepared and sent back to the kitchen, where the issue was quickly resolved. It wasn't a terrible mistake but a mistake nonetheless. It was a busy night, and I checked in with the server who told me about the problem, and I said "Let's buy them dessert" as a way to compensate for our error. It was a pretty standard response, but the server, who was equally busy, heard "Let's buy them dinner." Well, at the end of the evening, the host walked up to me and thanked me profusely for my generosity—which seemed a bit disproportionate to me at the time. Of course, eventually, I figured it all out and realized that we needed to have more specific systems in place to ensure that our responses to errors were proportionate. Good intentions only go so far!

Mike nods in agreement after I tell him my story. But he sees a silver lining: "I'd rather have them go that way once, I'd rather have everybody on the support team do that once, because it's a pretty low cost, and I know they'll make it up in the other stuff, if that makes sense."

From day one, FreshBooks has required every hire—from members of the executive team to the software engineers—to work in customer service for one month so that they can learn firsthand about customers and their needs. If you're someone who feels that's beneath you, you're not going to fit into their culture.

"In that first week, you learn about our values, you learn about our product, you learn about our customers, and you start answering the phones. In week two you start taking calls. By the time you leave that period, you understand the product, customer, and culture. A big part of that is you are taught by rock stars. You know them, they're around. You can't look down on them after you leave [training] because they were there for you when you didn't know anything."

How many companies do you know where members of the executive team answer phones for a month and the founder calls the customer service team "rock stars"? I ponder this as I realize I've known few corporate leaders with the patience or emotional intelligence to answer customer complaints on a daily basis. It's one thing to get into the weeds for a few days or a week, but, in my own experience, I find it challenging to dig in consistently every day, especially when there are so many other distractions while you're trying to run a business. Passion for customer service is almost like muscle memory—it needs to be practiced regularly to maintain it.

TAKING CARE OF THE TEAM

While it's debatable whether empathy can be taught, what I've heard over and over from the people I interviewed for this book is that empathy is certainly less likely to come from workers who are treated poorly. If you want outstanding customer service, you've got to offer outstanding employee service. Whether that's expressed in official policies such as servant leadership or simply practiced from the top down, it's imperative to treat all employees with respect.

As Mike says, "You can't treat people like shit and expect them to treat others well. My philosophy is take care of the team, the team takes care of the customers, and customers take care of you. I think that is fundamental to a lot of the things that follow. I can't say I necessarily knew that's how I thought about it when I started, but pretty soon I wrote that down, and I'm doing my best to live by it."

I realize that he's just described what people in my industry call the circle of hospitality, which includes the employees, the guests, and the shareholders, so I explain it to him. Unsurprisingly, he doesn't believe it's just a concept in the hospitality industry.

"I think every business has to balance these things. The thing that took root for me was when somebody said unless a decision balances all three, it's not a durable decision and will ultimately become undone."

NUTS AND BOLTS THE FRESHBOOKS WAY

The FreshBooks workspace is designed for "the three Cs:" collaboration, connectedness, and collisions. As Mike gave me a tour of his company, I gradually understood what this meant. There are no individual offices, except for Mike's (which, as previously mentioned, is entirely made of glass and purposefully located near the restrooms so that people can easily stop by for a chat).

The design helps connect employees to one another, he says. He wants employees to be visible and not to "feel like they're working for some mystery individual off in some ivory tower somewhere."

This connectedness is also fostered by the outer meeting rooms, also made of glass, so you can always easily find the people you need. Mike says he got the idea when he heard about the way Michael Bloomberg held open, public meetings when he was the mayor of New York City and decided he wanted to have open meetings as well.

Collaboration is cultivated by having lots of desks together in some areas without any kind of barrier between people. That way, he says, employees can spin around and chat when it's important.

Collisions happen in the kitchen, where every employee goes for coffee, lunch, and weekly meetings where Mike talks about the values of the company and shares stories about employees who have "made the values real." In addition to that public recognition, employees can be recognized for their work with a $25 gift card, which can be awarded anytime by any employee. Mike says it's not the amount of money that's important—it's the recognition.

"You can call that a 'program,' but for me it's wanting to reward and recognize the behaviors you want perpetuated. Create the conditions and reward and recognize the behaviors you want perpetuated. If you want great service, reward and recognize great service. If you want great cost cutting, reward and recognize great cost cutting."

As Mike says, "I didn't realize it, but we've been building a culture that's egalitarian. I think it's really important in service culture. If the service team feels like they're less important than other departments, I don't think you get the best from them."

THE VALUE OF MILLENNIALS

Retaining employees is good for a company's bottom line, but millennials won't stay if they feel their values are not respected in the corporate culture. In fact, a 2016 Gallup report on the millennial generation reveals that 21 percent of millennials say they've changed jobs within the past year, which is more than three times the number of non-millennials who report the same. Gallup estimates that millennial turnover costs the US economy $30.5 billion annually.[12]

This means that at most companies training goes on nonstop and institutional knowledge keeps disappearing. Mike says that to keep this generation engaged and loyal, your organization must be mission-driven or the problems of retention will continue.

This intuitive understanding of how to get the best out of younger employees is exactly what Crystal Kadakia and so many others have written about. In Kadakia's book, *The Millennial Myth: Transforming*

---

12 Adkins, Amy. "Millennials: The Job-Hopping Generation." Gallup.com. May 12, 2016.
  https://www.gallup.com/businessjournal/191459/millennials-job-hopping-generation.aspx.

Misunderstanding into Workplace Breakthroughs, she explains how important meaning, collaboration, and transparency are to her generation, and the benefits that companies can accrue by adapting to the new generational reality.

"The potential upside of letting go of our stereotypes, reestablishing understanding, and acting purposefully is immense," she writes. "Boomers, gen Xers, and millennials can form relationships where knowledge is transferred, productivity increases, and supportive community is built. . . . We can feel more empowered ourselves, knowing that we are not just doing what we have always done, but are doing the right things."[13]

Mike may not have consciously realized what he was doing, but FreshBooks's emphasis on collaboration, connectedness, meaning, recognition, and reward is exactly what appeals to millennials, who make up 74 percent of his total employees and most of the customer service team. The company's workspace seems particularly attuned to millennial desires and working styles. Regardless of whether Mike designed the company (and its office) this way on purpose, company cultures that reflect the values of millennials pay off, as Kadakia notes in her book. Unlike the majority of companies with a high percentage of millennials, Mike claims FreshBooks has a 93 percent retention rate.[14]

Given that millennials will be affecting and changing the culture of an increasing number of companies as more and more baby boomers retire, I wanted to hear more of Mike's thoughts about appealing to this cohort. Like so many people—from researchers and career experts to others profiled in this book—Mike says refocusing on values and meaning in the workplace is essential to doing so.

13 Crystal Kadakia, *The Millennial Myth*. (Oakland, CA: Berrett-Koehler Publishers, Inc., 2017), 8.

14 Clifford, Catherine. "How One Company Keeps Millennial Employees from Quitting." CNBC. com. September 19, 2016. https://www.cnbc.com/2016/09/19/how-one-company-keeps-millennial-employees-from-quitting.html.

"Human beings want meaning. I think the difference with more recent generations is they're not going to settle for a job that pays well as a reason to get in and do a good job every day. They need more. Maybe they don't practice religion anymore so what they choose to apply themselves to needs to matter. They've got to find meaning in this world."

Warming up to the subject, he continues. "When you're gen X, you're just glad to be employed because it [the economy] was shitty for a while. Before that you were the company person. Nowadays people think, 'I have lots of choices, I applied myself. Why the hell should I work for you?' In a world where your workforce can go wherever the hell it wants whenever the hell it wants, what they're seeking is meaning."

As we continue to talk about millennials' search for meaning in their work, Mike tells me he's found it's not just millennials—everyone, regardless of age, wants meaning in their work. He then relays a story about visiting a good friend of his, who was a very successful insurance salesman at the time. Mike was disturbed when he heard how cynical and jaded his friend was about work, so he asked him if he'd ever felt like he had a mission. The friend rolled his eyes and shook his head no. Disappointed in his friend, Mike told him he was being shallow and urged him to start his own business, which he did.

"He's working on it now. I connected him with another guy. They're almost getting into their third year, but I see him working and I see him motivated. If I asked him about work now, he would be genuinely excited. He'd never experienced that before. My point is, it's not just age. It's about the conditions. I think there are so many people who haven't had the benefit of seeing how much better it can be if you create the right conditions. It's in all of us [to do so]."

In fact, he's dismayed when he sees how many of his peers consider work a virtual prison: "I realize I'm living in another world. Toronto is a big city, but I hate hanging out with my best friends [and talking about work] because none of them cares about their jobs the way I do. Some of them are very successful, but I don't know how they get up in the morning. There's a lot of that attitude still going around, but generationally, expectations are changing."

THE FUTURE OF CUSTOMER SERVICE

As a tech company, FreshBooks understands the power of social media as well as its challenges and opportunities. An early adopter of Twitter, using it as a service tool to get and give instant feedback, Mike is well aware how social media influences a company's reputation—either positively or negatively.

"A lot of businesses think of social media as a risk. I think that's insane in the world where social media is today. You don't have a choice anymore. It's all wide open all the time. So you better be good. I think this is what's forcing businesses to take customer service seriously, what's forcing them to say, 'We have to solve this service thing because we're getting hammered on social media and everyone is hearing about it.'"

And then, taking the words out of my mouth, he continues:

"You're one recorded phone call away from being an internet nightmare, or one flight away from having your people drag somebody off a plane. Folks, this is all service, it's all hospitality. You can't get away from it anymore, and the leaders can't ignore it. How do you deal with this? The answer is culture. The answer is service."

FreshBooks, Mike says, came "baked"—by which I think he means prepared—for this new era because of its unwavering commitment to customer service and its employees. But if companies haven't yet made outstanding service a priority, they're going to have to "reculture" that part of their business quickly or they're not going to be around much longer.

Another tech company that he sees continuing to excel in the future is the elephant in everyone's room, Amazon. I can hear respect and also a bit of fear in his voice as he talks about Jeff Bezos.

"Look at Jeff Bezos. It's very interesting what he does. It's going to be on time and it's going to be fast. Amazon is a terrifying company. They're going to suck the life out of so many other categories and products, to the point of having no choice. But they're doing such a good job. It's a scary future in a world where it's basically impossible to imagine how you compete because monopolies start to emerge. They've set an expectation that they're fulfilling. People are growing up thinking, 'I push a button, I get a thing in no time.' Then you call up [another] company and get shitty service and you think, 'Why ever deal with them?' This century, they're stone ages. You are from the fucking stone ages if you offer terrible service."

FRESHBOOKS'S RECIPE FOR SUCCESS

Of all the companies profiled in this book, FreshBooks has probably given the most thought to matching its vision and values with those of the millennial generation. It's no surprise that FreshBooks is in the top five favorite places to work in various polls year after year, receiving recognitions such as being named in 2017 as one of the "Best Workplaces in Technology" by Great Place to Work Canada. That said, their recipe for success really isn't contrived, based on following a protocol or list of "ingredients": it shows itself in its everyday operations. There is very little about FreshBooks that is designed or determined in a traditional corporate manner. Mike has developed a set of values rather than a rulebook to guide the company, and his employees accept his vision.

You might say, "Well, I know myself, and I am not that kind of leader so what can I take away from FreshBooks's lessons?" I think there is actually a lot of useful information you can take from FreshBooks, as long as you believe that Mike's approach to employees and the workplace is valuable:

1. Physical space matters. Think about the nature of the floor plan—open spaces and collaborative glass meeting rooms—all of which are becoming more standard in the modern workplace. However, just making collaborative spaces isn't enough. If you fail to integrate the other essential pieces of the FreshBooks puzzle, it's the same death by a thousand pricks.

2. Everyone likes to be positively recognized for what they do. People at the bottom of the pecking order work very hard. Those usually unsung "Rock Stars" are often what can make or break a company. It's no coincidence that there's excellent customer service at FreshBooks, where everyone starts out as a rock star. Another way employees are recognized, a $25 gift card, doesn't seem like much, but it can go a long way toward making someone feel good about themselves and their job.

3. People want to be allowed to solve problems without a manager looking over their shoulder. Do some employees go overboard and make mistakes? Yep. But Mike would rather employees be too generous than not generous enough.

Great leaders such as Mike recognize that filtering for empathetic employees requires additional effort but pays off in the long run. Just as important is a company's environment, which must be supportive and accountable to its employees. But perhaps most importantly, the culture has to be genuine. As Mike explains, genuine corporate culture gives a company purpose, which inspires its employees, which translates directly to extraordinary customer service. And great profits to boot.

CHAPTER 6

BROOKLYN BREWERY:
EDUCATION

"I tell them all the same thing I was saying thirty years ago, which is, 'Look, you've got to develop real customers, people who are really committed to us and people who we're committed to, and help them build their business with the Brooklyn brands.' That philosophy was developed thirty years ago and is still at the core of what we're doing now." —**STEVE HINDY**

When you speak with Steve Hindy, founder of Brooklyn Brewery, his passion and commitment to his business and the world around him are clear. Steve is a great storyteller, which isn't surprising given that he was a writer long before he started Brooklyn Brewery. He began his career as a war correspondent for the Associated Press, and after spending more than five years covering wars and assassinations throughout the Middle East, he finally returned to New York after one too many close calls. Fond memories of sampling extraordinary home brews returned with him, and he and his business partner Tom Potter went on to develop one of the first craft beer companies in the Northeast by founding Brooklyn Brewery in 1988.

From Steve's perspective, Brooklyn was and remains a natural fit for his brand. Traditionally home to many immigrants and artists, the city had a long history of hosting mom-and-pop bars with home-brewed beer long before Brooklyn Brewery came along and reoriented the playing field. In fact, at the turn of the last century, Brooklyn itself was home to forty-five breweries, including eleven on one twelve-block stretch of the Williamsburg neighborhood. This amounted to a significant share of the nation's production. But Prohibition took its toll and, over time, the dynamics of the neighborhoods changed. By the mid-1970s beer production had all but ceased in Brooklyn.

So, it's not surprising that Steve pursued a modest vision of trying to sell his beer door to door in the early days. As he hit the streets, it did not take long for him to recognize that most consumers neither cared about nor understood craft beer. Steve knew that it wasn't the consumer's fault. The beer that he and Potter had developed, Brooklyn Lager, represented a completely new approach to brewing. Without knowing or planning it, Steve was a "disruptive innovator" in the brewing sector.

While the Budweisers of the world were off selling to the masses, Steve believed that there was an overlooked market segment interested in a more sophisticated product. So while the bigger players were looking in the other direction, he quietly but assuredly began making inroads into the market. As a result of his new product and approach, Brooklyn Brewery decided to build its own distribution network. Initially Steve focused on introducing and delivering the Brooklyn Brewery brand, but later he added other craft beers such as Sierra Nevada, Dog Street, and Harpoon, as well as beer from international brewing hotspots such as Belgium, Germany, and the United Kingdom to his distribution network.

Ironically, at first it was harder to sell the brew locally than it was to sell it in Asia and Europe. This indicated just how revolutionary

Steve's beer was in Brooklyn.

"From the very beginning . . . we had people coming to us from Sweden, from Japan, from Brazil, from France, saying, 'Wow, we tried this beer in New York. We don't have anything like this in our country. We want to import the beer to Japan or wherever.' I don't know if I said this, but what I was thinking was, are you kidding me? I can't sell this shit in Brooklyn. Are you crazy?"

At the time, the Brewery was so cash-strapped that they agreed to work with amateur distributors, such as a Japanese oil executive and a Swedish SAS pilot. It sounds pretty crazy, but this strategy slowly paid off, and Brooklyn Brewery made inroads into international markets—almost unintentionally. Today, the Carlsberg Group is their distributor in Northern Europe while Kirin is starting to brew Brooklyn Lager in Japan. Brooklyn Brewery is currently the largest independent exporter of craft beer in the US and it continues to expand its reach across the globe.

Although Steve had created a distribution company, in 2003 he realized that in order to grow the brewing side of the business, they needed to sell the distribution business. Brooklyn Brewery had been around for about fifteen years at that point and had established a significant, if nonthreatening, market foothold. At the time of the sale in 2003, they sold about forty-eight thousand barrels annually of the beer they brewed. Today, through a distributor, Brooklyn Brewery sells more than three hundred thousand barrels of it annually, half of which is exported. This phenomenal growth has challenged the organization to evolve from a small group of passionate beer aficionados to an international organization staffed by people who must learn about and then embrace the Brooklyn Brewery culture. To do this, Steve focuses on three key elements to maintain Brooklyn Brewery's success: training, corporate culture, and community.

TRAINING: PART ONE

With Steve at the helm, Brooklyn Brewery delivered its first case of "unusually dark," hoppy ale to Brooklyn's neighborhood bars in 1988. (It was unusual because at the time, the vast majority of Americans drank mass-produced beers like Budweiser, which are paler in color.) These days you can walk into a bar in just about any city in the United States and try a variety of local brews, but that wasn't the case in the late '80s. Back then, Steve and Tom were the renegades who had not only developed a different kind of beer, but also a completely new way to market it. Although they believed their beer deserved the same respect given to a bottle of pinot noir, they also knew that the only way to get people to take that idea seriously was to educate them about beer. This insight, that people had to be educated about beer in the same way they had been educated about wine, was and is the first element in the training process and a foundation of the Brooklyn Brewery brand.

Step one in educating their new employees was teaching them the history of beer and its many styles, from Irish stout to Bavarian hefe-weizen. Before Brooklyn Brewery, consumers had limited scope and style expectations for beer; the term "craft beer" was not a part of the common lexicon. With this understanding in mind, the ultimate goal was established: to cultivate long-term clients, not just "one and done." The idea was that when business owners saw a Brooklyn Brewery sales person coming, they would know they weren't going to be asked to take on the same old beer in a "new" package. Instead, the salesperson would help an owner increase his business by getting his customers excited about trying innovative, flavorful beers.

"We really went to school on how the wine guys sell wine. We told our sales people, 'We want you to be essentially consultants for your customers and you help them build a beer list that makes sense in their restaurant or their bar that fits with their menu,'" recalls Steve.

TRAINING: PART TWO

You might think selling beer is not very complex. After all, it's every-where, from college keggers to summer barbecues. This may be true, yet a significant, dedicated effort is still required to ensure that the torch of the company's vision is carried with every case. Currently, Brooklyn Brewery employs about 115 full-time and 60 part-time people. New hires all go through the same training, called "Beer School," where each salesperson becomes a "brand ambassador" and attends a three-day training program on the history of beer in general and Brooklyn Brewery in particular.

Going to this school sounds like a lot more fun than working physics equations or studying the periodic table. Students at Beer School sample beer at a dinner cooked by the company's brewmaster, Garrett Oliver, or the company's personal chef, and learn how to pair beer with a variety of food, just like a sommelier. The student employees also read copies of Steve's book, *The Craft Beer Revolution: How a Band of Microbrewers is Transforming the World's Favorite Drink*, and Oliver's book, *The Brewmaster's Table: Discovering the Pleasures of Real Beer with Real Food*, before rounding out the syllabus with *The Oxford Companion to Beer*, an encyclopedia of beer for laypeople, which Oliver edited.

Steve's commitment to creating a meaningful service experi-ence for his business-to-business customers has been driven by his investment in training his sales force. Remember, in the late 1980s and early 1990s, few people knew what "craft beer" was and very few people had ever tasted dark and hoppy beer. Therefore, it was essential that Brooklyn Brewery employees educate each new customer. Steve recognized that just as Americans had become excited about trying new wines and incorporating them into their lifestyles, many would be just as intrigued about making beer an important element of the dining experience.

Steve believed people would buy the new style of beer if they understood it, so he took a chance and printed beer lists to accompany menus in local restaurants around Brooklyn. His hunch was validated when Florence Fabricant of the *New York Times* wrote a large article in 1993 titled, "Candlelight. Fine Food. Waiter, the Beer List!" At that point, Steve knew that educating customers about a whole new beverage category was a recipe for success. While it may seem obvious in retrospect, Steve was a revolutionary. He captured an idea about leadership and customer service that has served Brooklyn Brewery well for over thirty years.

At the end of the day, Steve says one of his greatest pleasures is "changing the world in a small way by selling good beer and turning people onto good beer." While that might sound like a simple idea, it would never have worked without him first realizing the importance of educating his workforce and the greater community about beer.

A COMMUNITY BREWS IN BROOKLYN

It's impossible to overstate how important a sense of community is to Brooklyn Brewery—both inside and outside the organization. The process of building a tight-knit, loyal group of employees starts at the table at Beer School, where employees share meals and build relationships in the same way communities have for generations, through food, drink, and conversation. The tradition of welcoming people and developing a nurturing environment doesn't stop there, either; it permeates all aspects of the company. To illustrate this point, Steve recounts a great story to me. One time the brewers were developing a new type of beer, and he took a keg home. What to do with it?

"I thought, 'I'll invite the marketing department to my house.'" Twenty people came, and I did a barbecue. I slow-cooked our pork butt and they had a great time. . . . Then, of course the brewers said,

'Well, shit. The marketing department gets to come to your cookout and we don't?' I said, 'Well the marketing guys didn't kill the keg, so maybe I should have you guys over.' The brewers came and that was like twenty-five more people. They killed the keg in the first half hour. Now I'm on the hook. Now I've got to bring the logistics and the admin and the warehouse people. . . . Then I know our out of state sales people are going to be knocking on the door."

The truth is that Steve loves all this. For him, these get-togethers maintain a personal connection that he believes is vital to the organization's success. "You know, you've got to make an extra effort if you're going to maintain that sense of intimacy and connection with people," he says. He puts into action his belief that great leaders must stay connected to the core business practices that drove success in the early days. In Brooklyn Brewery's case, that means staying true to its mission and caring for fellow employees. Steve accepts and embraces the idea that he needs to be personally accountable to his employees, no matter how large the organization becomes, whether he's selling beer to a local bar or a restaurant halfway across the world.

BUILDING COMMUNITY ON THE OUTSIDE

Community engagement is another aspect of the Brooklyn Brewery heritage that has continued to evolve and expanded exponentially over the years. An early example of such engagement was the company's creation of a local music festival called the Brooklyn Lager Band Search in 1989. Designed to highlight unsigned bands in the area, the festival gave away awards to rock, world beat, and jazz groups that played in local venues. In 2017, the company hosted a party in Brooklyn called Brooklyn Brewery Beer Mansion and more than one thousand people attended. It featured live music, art, local food, and, of course, beer. The Brewery has hosted similar events in Chicago, Philadelphia, London, and Paris. Though the events are sponsored by Brooklyn Brewery, they are definitely not beer events. As far as Steve is concerned, it's all about building community by infusing energy into local businesses; selling more beer in the process is just gravy.

Steve recalls another early example of building community bonds that aligned with the culture of the Brewery. He and some colleagues decided that an old-school blues bar in New York City called Tramps would be a perfect venue for a special beer event. So Steve and one of his salesmen approached the owner, Terry Dunn, and told him they wanted to take over Tramps for one night to bring in Michael Jackson, the world's foremost beer expert (not the singer). Dunn thought they were crazy and was certain it would never work.

After a lot of back and forth, he finally agreed to their request and listed it along with the regular acts as "Michael Jackson Live at Tramps." In the fine print, the flyer explained that *this* Michael Jackson was the beer expert, not the King of Pop. Regardless, on the night of the event, there was a packed house. Dunn was flabbergasted when he realized Tramps was filled with people who had *purposefully* come to hear the beer expert. (He was also delighted to get a cut of the proceeds.) It was a turning point for Steve because he realized the brand could be a beacon in the community, not just a beer label.

Steve admits there have been challenges in maintaining culture through significant transitions in the company's evolution, especially when he sold the distribution part of the company in 2003. At that inflection point, the Brewery's hand-picked staff was no longer dealing directly with bar and restaurant owners, who now had to place orders with a larger distributor. The new distributor didn't really know anything about Brooklyn, the history of Brooklyn Brewery, or even craft beer. Steve recognized this change in relationships would require a whole new focus on the basics.

As Steve describes it, "I always told our sales managers who were working with the distributors, 'Look, find out and identify the salespeople at the distributorship who understand what we are, who understand better beer, understand craft beer. I'd rather you worked with five out of fifty people. I'd rather start with them than try to convert all fifty of them from day one.' It was similar to the philosophy I had early on, when I'd rather have ten really good customers than one hundred people who just buy the beer once. You kind of fish where the fish are, which is pretty basic to selling."

Social media is playing an increasing role in keeping the Brewery relevant to a new generation of beer drinkers. Thanks to Milton Glaser, the legendary graphic artist, the Brooklyn Brewery's logo is already iconic. (Back in 1988, Glaser agreed to waive his normal fee in exchange for equity in the company and has since designed many of its labels, keeping his office well-supplied in fresh beer.)

Other events such as the Brooklyn Lager Band Search and the Art of Fine Beer Contest—originally created by Steve as a way to offer prizes for the best painting, drawing, or poem on a Brooklyn Brewery bar coaster—also continue to spread the word about the Brewery as artists vie for the chance of being featured on a Brooklyn Brewery bar coaster. These days there are fifteen people in the marketing department, and Steve is convinced that social media has magnified all of the company's early grassroots efforts so that the impact of what they're doing now is far greater than it was.

Speaking of impact, Steve reiterates that giving back to the community is the key to the company's marketing strategy—and is undoubtedly responsible for its financial success.

Each year, the Brewery donates free beer to hundreds of nonprofits and special events in New York that celebrate what Steve calls "the native or creative culture." The result is enormous goodwill—and invaluable positive publicity. "I can't go anywhere without people saying, By the way, I don't know if you know this, but you guys have been donating beer to my dance company's fundraiser for like twenty years. If you went out and tried to buy this kind of recognition, the New York media would be happy to take millions and millions of dollars from you, but you might not get shit out of it. The way we've done it, I think has been very effective and like I said, it's been completely magnified by social media. And, it's authentic."

SPREADING BROOKLYN'S
CULTURE ACROSS THE GLOBE

So how does Brooklyn Brewery take its unique spin across the world while at the same time remaining true to its values? Steve says it's simple: hire the right people. They can bring the same passion and excitement about the brand to London or Paris or Stockholm. For him, it's all about transplanting the company's commitment to local community to other places by going back to basics, spotlighting local craft beers, and celebrating the local culture in whatever city they're in. Of course, they'll feature Brooklyn Brewery brews, but more importantly, the partnerships focus on showcasing the best local craft beers as well.

Steve has also benefitted from the rise of the Brooklyn borough's brand—which, of course, he had a hand in building. "I don't have to tell you; it's quite amazing that Brooklyn [the borough] has evolved as this maker and creator of culture. In so many places you go now in the world, people say this is our 'Brooklyn neighborhood.' In order to infuse this same energy into the Brooklyn Brewery brand, we focused on restaurants and bars that really are committed to us, not just a 'Beer of the Month club' kind of mentality." Steve's consistent, laser-like focus on community and culture are typical of his leadership style.

Steve believes part of what makes Brooklyn Brewery unique is its dedication to its employees, and he still takes great pleasure in recognizing when employees go the extra mile. He told me he had just sent a "heiogram" to the team responsible for a successful event the night before. Yet, unlike some other notable entrepreneurs, Steve wouldn't describe Brooklyn Brewery as a cult—at least not formally. Instead, he revels in the fine quality of employees who continually strengthen the business.

And fine they are. Steve says there is no shortage of high-quality people who are interested in being a part of the iconic Brooklyn company. "There are so many educated people who come down the financial world sinkhole or even the legal world or the corporate world who just can't wait to get away from that and want to work for a small independent company. I don't feel a need to screen people. The kind of people we want apply to us in great numbers, and it's really a matter of choosing among ten fantastic applicants for every job here."

He makes it sounds so easy, almost like an accident, which is par for the course. If nothing else, Steve is a cool guy. Yet it's obvious that Brooklyn Brewery has made a purposeful effort to make sure everybody in the organization is drinking from the same Kool-Aid—or, perhaps, keg.

In fact, this sensibility directly relates to Steve's perception of millennials, who are both employed by the Brewery and the principal consumers of the product. What makes the Brewery different from many other organizations doing the same thing is that the company's commitment to community-giving and sustainability, for example, happened organically when Steve first got started. It was never something adopted in a boardroom out of a perceived sense that it would make a good PR campaign. In fact, Steve claims that these efforts benefit Brooklyn Brewery on several levels. Most important, he feels strongly about the Donations Program and its ability to help community efforts and also speak to employees and consumers—and, according to Steve, drive potential new employees to the organization.

Along with a chorus of others, Steve recognizes that authenticity and meaning is a critical component in attracting great millennial employees and keeping them.

CUSTOMER SERVICE FOR ALL

In the end, I'm struck by how innovative Brooklyn Brewery's customer service model is. Steve didn't instill traditional customer service tools or practices at Brooklyn Brewery. Instead, he identified a need in the market and addressed it while remaining true to his training, community, and culture. This leadership approach, one that couldn't be further away from the traditional "command and control" formula, has fostered extraordinary growth and loyalty from his employees and customers. And considerable profits.

As we close our conversation and I'm pondering this realization, Steve excitedly tells me about his plans for the evening. They completely exemplify his unique approach.

"We did this series at the Brewery called "War Correspondents at the Brooklyn Brewery," where I interview war reporters. Tonight we have Victor Blue from the *New York Times* and *The New Yorker*. That event will attract journalists, students, and foreign policy nuts. It raises money for an organization called RISC, Reporters Instructed in Saving Colleagues. It trains freelance war reporters in first aid and gets them medical kits. It was started by Sebastian Junger and my daughter. That's also a way that I kind of keep in touch with my roots as a foreign correspondent and I think it's also an effective way to market the Brewery as a thought leader in something that really matters to me."

BROOKLYN BREWERY'S RECIPE FOR SUCCESS

Brooklyn Brewery with Steve at the helm proves that a well-oiled, highly stylized corporate construct for leadership is not a prerequisite for success. In fact, to the contrary, Steve excels because of his consistent passion for the product, the community of people that make up his organization, and his love of Brooklyn. It's an honest and genuine approach that has led to extraordinary growth without sacrificing the early core cultural values that made the Brewery successful in the first place.

For Steve, success is a pretty straightforward recipe:

1. TRAINING—Give your employees a sense of purpose that goes beyond the basics. It's easy for a leader to provide the "blocking and tackling" required to sell a product. The bigger challenge, and one that Brooklyn Brewery has faced exceptionally well, is to develop and nurture passion for a product. This takes time, a sense of purpose, and consistent messaging from the day of hire and through every event that's sponsored by the company. It's an especially thoughtful approach.

2. CULTURE—Like training, the culture cannot be faked. In fact, culture and training are woven together in many ways to ensure that the brand message is consistent. Accountable leadership embraces the torch of culture and considers it in every action, ensuring a consistent message and hands-on approach.

3. COMMUNITY—Genuine leadership cannot stop at the warehouse door. Leaders must create the time and brain space to engage with the broader community, both to express the brand's appreciation to it and to reinforce the legitimacy of the company's culture. In the case of Brooklyn Brewery, each effort not only results in benefits to the brand but also reinforces employees' pride.

Steve sums it up: "You know, when I started in '88, imports were 2 percent of the US market and I thought that was the segment, the niche that we were competing against. What's happened in the last thirty years is imports have grown to be 15 percent of the US market and now craft beer, if you count the craft breweries that have been bought by the big guys, it's actually about 16 percent of the US market. We really have revolutionized and changed the American beer market."

THE PRAGMATISTS

Jerrod Melman
(Lettuce Entertain You Enterprises)

Richard Coraine
(Union Square Hospitality Group)

Mark Hoplamazian
(Hyatt Hotels)

The three insightful leaders profiled in this section all stepped into an established company. In doing so, they recognized the importance of keeping the values that originally differentiated the company from its competitors and the necessity of evolving to meet the needs of the current marketplace. In each case, they adapted existing practices and forged a new path forward to help their organizations compete with new competitors. They acknowledge that younger employees are changing workplace culture, but the pragmatists still maintain a laser-like focus on offering exceptional customer service. As a result, they have positioned their organizations for excellence today and for the foreseeable future.

CHAPTER 7

LETTUCE ENTERTAIN YOU: CONSISTENCY FOR THE BRAND AND THE CUSTOMER

"We're a very disciplined organization. We run restaurants well. People think of us as creative—and I do believe we possess creativity-but more importantly, we play good solid ball. Our costs are good. We surround ourselves with good people and we train them well . . . not a lot of fancy stuff, just the basics. And, we work very hard." —Richard Melman

---

Richard Melman and Jerry Orzoff opened their first Chicago restaurant, R. J. Grunts, at exactly 11:32 a.m., June 10, 1971. The fact that it's still operating more than forty-five years later is a testament not only to its self-proclaimed "funky, devil-may-care" décor, music, and vibe but also to a lot of hard work and leadership that ensures that the food tastes as good now as it did when it opened and in its early days. Come in on a random Thursday for pot roast, the fifty ingredient salad bar, and a giant chocolate malt, and you'll leave happily full.

R. J. Grunts was the first of more than 150 venues that have been opened and operated by Lettuce Entertain You Enterprises, or "Lettuce" as it is commonly referred to in the restaurant industry. The organization has grown to be the largest independent restaurant group in the country. R. J. Grunts counts other notable firsts too. When the original restaurant opened, it was one of the first restaurants in the country that focused as much on the ambience of the space as it did on the food.

Melman gave his subsequent restaurants names such as "Jonathan Livingston Seafood" and "Lawrence of Oregano," establishing himself as the master of the kind of casual restaurant that exuded the laid-back, hippy vibe of the 1970s. But while the vibe may have been loose and easy, the operations were deliberate and evolved. At the same time, Melman wanted to expand his vision, so he soon ventured into the world of fine dining. In 1976, he took over the iconic Pump Room, a Chicago classic that first opened its doors in 1938—and is still in operation today though now operating under the name Booth One.

Early on as his restaurant empire expanded, Melman brought other talented restaurant professionals in as partners. These partners have equity in individual restaurants or groups of restaurants and serve as the owner-operators of the business. The philosophy of partnership has continued to this day, making sure those who are loyal to Lettuce are rewarded in kind.

Today a new generation of Melmans is picking up where Richard left off as he now focuses more on strategy and less on operations. The kids are establishing a new pattern of operations and hospitality while continuing to embrace the formula that led to the company's success more than forty years ago. So much so, in fact, that the Lettuce empire now has a foothold in seven states and Washington, DC.

Jerrod Melman, Richard's middle child, began working in the restaurant business as a teenager. He has worked just about every job, from cashier to manager, learning many valuable lessons along the way.

With his siblings, he opened Chicago's now famous HUB 51 in 2008 and has continued to expand the Lettuce brand and its relentless focus on hospitality.

I meet Jerrod in his downtown Chicago basement office on a typically chilly spring day. There's nothing fancy here; you'd never know it was the beehive of a large restaurant group. He is running late for our meeting, just finishing another conversation over at one of the restaurants, and it occurs to me that the restaurants are as much his office as this small room in which I'm waiting for him.

Finally he arrives. One of the first things I notice about Jerrod is that he exudes a natural ease and confidence. He validates this feeling as we begin to discuss his perspective on the business.

THE LETTUCE PHILOSOPHY

At the core of the Lettuce philosophy is *caring* for both customers and employees. Because of this, there is an emphasis throughout the organization on empathy and action. That means making the word "yes" the first word out of people's mouths throughout the organization; not "maybe," not "no,"—but "yes."

As he explains, "For us, a lot of our teaching and our culture is about caring, and a lot of it is about one word, which is 'yes.' Wanting to say 'yes' to people, wanting to be giving. . . , [It's] how you take care of yourself and how you take care of your coworkers. If you are feeling really lousy, it's going to be hard to be giving."

He is particularly passionate about the idea of saying "yes" to employees as well as customers. He recalls stories his parents told him about working for owners and bosses who treated employees badly. In response, his father was determined to create a culture with a different environment, one that hinged on people taking care of one another.

"If our philosophy is based on 'yes,' then that also means saying yes to the people that work around us," says Jerrod. "If you're managing, and you need a weekend off for something that's important, wanting to say 'yes' is a part of that."

Another core principle at Lettuce is accountability and a genuine belief in leadership through example. As Jerrod puts it, "It's not enough to say you believe in [being accountable]. Leaders have to walk the talk at every level." He says he learned this value as he worked alongside managers who showed him the importance of taking responsibility and not passing the buck.

"I grew up with leaders that, when something's on the floor, you pick it up. I hate stuff on the floor. I don't need to say that to people every day, but if [I pick up things] every day, I believe other people will follow. If I didn't believe it was important to have a clean restaurant, I don't know that other people would care, either." In other words, effective leaders need to set the right example to show they are accountable to *all* the employees they manage.

A "WELL-BAKED" CULTURE

Lettuce's steady growth over the years has presented a new set of challenges (albeit good ones). One of the most significant is preserving the company's culture. So how does it maintain a unified culture when its home office is in Chicago but other venues are scattered across the country, in places as far apart as Scottsdale, Minneapolis, Santa Monica, and Washington, DC? Jerrod says a unified vision is maintained by carefully communicating the original culture of the company and then encouraging each partner to add his or her vision into their particular venture. This resulting blend, says Jerrod, is what's so exciting and special about Lettuce.

"All our restaurants take on their own subcultures, and they have their own feel that sort of complements, or supplements the overarching Lettuce culture. So, part of how we do it is just built into our structure. Partner businesses have standard things that are part of Lettuce, and then they also have freedom in what they're doing to create, to use the products they want, to use the uniforms they want. Whatever it might be, that's how we create our culture." This philosophy allows for significant flexibility but also creates accountability to the overall brand, he says.

To build a positive culture, Lettuce has designed a system that emphasizes both communication and the possibility for advancement. To do this, each restaurant has an evolving, yet formalized training system in place. The system has seen many changes throughout the company's evolution and has been "reimagined" or restructured multiple times.

In Lettuce culture, knowledge about the food is a priority, since it instills confidence in the servers and makes it easier for them to recommend certain dishes. Thus, if you ask a server in any Lettuce restaurant how spicy the chili is or what their favorite item on the menu is, you're not going to get a blank stare and responses such as the following, "Well, people seem to like the sea bass. I've never tried it, but people who order it seem to." Servers in Lettuce venues taste the whole menu and have been doing so since R. J. Grunts opened.

"When my dad started the company, I think probably fewer restaurants did that than do today, but he believed, and we believe, that if you're going to sell something, you have to know it," says Jerrod. "You have to believe in it. It's a huge cost to have every employee in our restaurants taste all the food but it's important to us. It's important that they have the knowledge and the confidence to sell something, to believe in something."

Jerrod readily admits that he cannot measure the ROI of having every server taste every item on the menu and that it's definitely expensive in the short run. However, he says the cost doesn't matter because he firmly believes the practice leads to a better guest and employee experience—which ultimately leads to better financial performance.

"I don't know exactly how to quantify the return on it. I wouldn't even know where to begin to study some of those things, but some of them just are, 'This is what we feel is right.'" The company's decades of success certainly seem to validate this belief.

TALK TO ME

Of course, it's not enough to establish a great culture and then let it run on autopilot. Any company that "walks the walk" and truly believes in hospitality needs other tools to make sure the overarching culture manifests itself on a daily basis. According to Jerrod, the most important thing Lettuce does is keep lines of communication open from top to bottom.

"A lot of great ideas come from people who are close to the guests. [To outsiders] it can look like spontaneous creation or whatever, but a lot of our ideas just come from listening and communicating with our guests."

In order to make it easy for the servers to stay in touch with senior management, the entire organization is required to use and review "motivational sheets." Even when the restaurant is at its busiest, servers write down ideas for managers, ranging from something as simple as asking for more forks to a suggestion to add fried chicken to the menu, since so many customers have asked for it. This ensures that communication lines stay open because it's then incumbent upon management to respond. Again, it's about walking the talk and listening not only to the guests but employees too.

He points to a recent example to make this point. A Lettuce restaurant in Washington, DC, had an unusually high bartender turnover. Since Washington, DC, is far from Lettuce's corporate headquarters and not directly exposed to the Lettuce culture, many of the protocols and procedures had become somewhat diluted, as Jerrod readily admits. It was clear something had to be done, but what? The team decided even more communication was needed in order to correct the course and solve the problem.

Now, "I am meeting with that team leader every Tuesday and Thursday, and it's clear what we are supposed to be talking about and what kinds of things need our attention," Jerrod says. "I have worked in restaurants my whole life. A successful restaurant is a group of people that are able to work toward the same thing, right or wrong, and change course accordingly."

Changing course is easier when there are communication systems in place that help people feel they're succeeding, that help them feel important, that encourage empathy, not punishment. These systems, he says, are essential to the organization's success.

"I've worked in restaurants that have great communication, [and] I've worked in restaurants that have lousy communication. As an employee you have to pick and choose where you are going to work. I think it's [about] having people that care enough to communicate at all levels."

He offers another example of how communication at every level was able to solve a major problem. One Lettuce restaurant was consistently placing emergency print orders for menus every Friday because they didn't have enough for dinner that night. As you can imagine, this is a major headache for the internal team responsible for getting menus printed in a timely, ordered way. There was, as Jerrod points out, a "short circuit" that needed to be addressed, since running out of menus is not good for business; customers tend to get cranky if they have to wait until another table has finished with the menus before they can get them.

The managers were clearly cutting things too closely, but instead of criticizing them for being shortsighted and disorganized, the leadership team beefed up their level of communication and examined *why* this kept happening at that particular venue, clearly demonstrating their belief that talking about problems and working out a solution together—not having one dictated from above—works best.

"Now we've got to just go back and *talk* to that team and say, 'Okay what is your process for changing menus and counting menus and ordering menus? Let's see if we can make this better because it's taxing the larger system.' It's okay if it happens every now and again. There will always be emergencies. That's not what we're trying to avoid. We're trying to avoid *consistent* emergencies."

CONSISTENCY IS HARD WORK!

At this point, you may be thinking, "All of this is fine when you've got motivated, hardworking employees. I've got some of those, but I've also got some slackers who only do the bare minimum and have no desire to accomplish more than that. How does this work with them?"

Jerrod argues that having a defined culture that stresses communication and empathy, along with ongoing training, is the foundation for creating cohesive, successful teams. This helps ensure that most employees inevitably integrate into the Lettuce system—a consistency of staff, if you will. It's not that all employees at Lettuce start out great, but having systems in place makes it obvious when someone is not participating or is disruptive to the team. When that happens, the company can deal with the problem on a case by case basis, recognizing that skill sets vary and not everyone is good at everything.

"In the menu [situation] I just talked about, I would say, 'Who's the closing manager on Thursday? What is the system in place to count menus?' Maybe they have a system, and they're just not using it. Maybe they don't, but we need to have a conversation about that before we can take any action."

Jerrod continues to stress the importance of consistency, starting with the food. After all, you're not going to order the pulled chicken nachos at Hub 51 if they come with guacamole, salsa, cheddar, and Oaxaca cheeses one day but green chili peppers, which you can't stand, another. The food has to *consistently* come out the way you love it or you'll go somewhere else.

This same approach applies to other aspects within the organization, from hiring to pre-shift meetings, which are at the same time every day and touch upon the same issues. "We know we have a process. It's not always perfect. It's always up for revision . . . but it is consistent."

MILLENNIALS

As the youngest person profiled in this book and a near-millennial himself, Jerrod, who is thirty-four, views millennials positively, with a few slight caveats.

"So, what I see, if we're going to talk about millennials, maybe their human interactions are lagging, or suffering . . . but I really think that their gravitation toward brands that have integrity, brands that treat their people well, brands that are transparent, I think that that is what's happening right now," he says.

Lettuce's care for employees up and down the organization as well as its emphasis on communication also reflect values important to millennials, as we've discussed previously. It's also, I think, a large part of the reason why Jerrod finds the current crop of employees similar to those in the past.

"Looking at a group of people working in a restaurant, fifteen years ago, versus today, do I think it's drastically different? No. I think a server in a restaurant twelve years ago, and a server in a restaurant now want, for the most part, the same things, right? They're drawn to either food, or the flexible schedule of it, or the ability to make money in real time and be in charge of your own destiny a little bit. . . . Maybe I'm completely missing something, but someone working in a restaurant ten years ago probably . . . [also wanted] to make money and to be treated in a way that is nice," Jerrod says.

The company's emphasis on training, feedback, and consistency in message is another reason millennials thrive at the Lettuce organization. As Jerrod says, no one expects a twenty-two-year-old manager to be "perfect" or excellent" right out of college, even after three months of training. But if the employee fits into the organization, he or she will work closely with the general manager, who will be giving constant feedback and asking what went well, and what didn't go well. In the end, it seems like the Lettuce system embodies millennials' values in many ways.

EVOLUTION

Now, the million-dollar question: How does Lettuce simultaneously evolve while staying true to its culture of empathy? Technology is ubiquitous. It affects the way customers find and report on their experiences (through such things as Yelp and TripAdvisor) and it can also influence the ways employees communicate. (We've all seen people staring into their phones when they're supposed to be working. These people may even be us!) This question is at the crux of the customer service challenge. So, how *do* organizations use technology to enhance the customer experience, not just create efficiencies?

To explore this issue, Jerrod and I started by talking about something near and dear to my heart: grocery shopping. We agree that the most enjoyable part of going to a grocery store is meandering through the aisles, looking for new products and finding the freshest ones. Our least favorite part? Like everyone else, we think waiting in line can suck the life out of you.

Jerrod wondered whether putting resources toward training and hiring—like the Walgreens "I see three" program, which was developed to avoid stores having more than two customers waiting in line, or borrowing parts of Amazon's efficiency model to reduce the checkout "pain point"—will ultimately win out in the retail environment. At the same time, he reflects on what the Lettuce restaurants do. "We treat technology like a tool. It's only as good as the people and the ideas we're using the technology for. It can't be just about our efficiency. It has to be about making the guests happier and delighting them and pleasing them." While retail and restaurants are not equivalent, it's not hard to imagine a time when consumers will use the same measurements around efficiency.

"If I'm [a grocery store], should I be working toward what Amazon's doing? A grocery store where you can go in, get your stuff, and it'll be tracked, and you can walk out, and they'll bill you, or take it right out of your account? Doesn't that seem logical?" asks Jerrod.

Yet while we agree that there are significant benefits to utilizing technology to reduce "pain points" as part of the transaction process, there are also risks. I asked him how he thought taking the human element out of the transaction would affect the long-term ability to provide outstanding customer service.

He agrees that even a grocery store can benefit from face to face interactions—he cites Wegmans as a model grocery store chain—and acknowledges the benefits of hospitality in the grocery store business as a differentiating factor. For him, like many of the companies profiled in the book, it all comes back to mission and keeping a laser focus on the customer.

As someone who grew up in front of a computer, he's not afraid to experiment with technology to enhance efficiencies inside and outside the Lettuce organization. The goal is for employees to "Do the behind the scenes tasks a little bit better to have more time for the things we think are important, like taking care of guests."

For instance, Lettuce now uses CareerBuilder to streamline its hiring process. Of course, a new management tool requires not only teaching all employees how to use it but also retraining, something that inevitably takes time and money. But he says the short-term costs are worth it. Any cost in time today is made up for by time savings tomorrow.

"We're increasingly folding technology in with the mindset of 'How do we improve our service to our guests?' It's not always about efficiency, though efficiency is often a byproduct of that. We're a company that's grown from one restaurant to 150 restaurants. I want to provide the same feel, but there's a lot more information coming in, so we're going to use technology to manage it."

Still, efficiency isn't the end-all-be-all. No matter what changes technology brings, Jerrod reiterates the importance of consistent leadership and a culture that prizes empathy in action and provides outstanding service to customers and employees alike.

LETTUCE ENTERTAIN YOU'S RECIPE FOR SUCCESS

There's no doubt that Jerrod Melman's calm, purposeful demeanor indicates both his personal style and Lettuce Entertain You Enterprise's approach. This restaurant group is built on a combination of thoughtful, innovative ideas and practical know-how. Much of Lettuce's success is derived from the fact that the leadership does the necessary work every day, and does it consistently. From Jerrod's perspective, the company is only as strong as its leaders' willingness to dig into the daily operations. There is no substitute for walking the floor of his business and simply picking up a stray piece of paper.

Being a model service company takes principles. These are the three that form Lettuce's foundation:

1. EMPATHY: Wake up every day with a willingness to say "yes"—to your employees, to your customers, and, perhaps most importantly, to yourself. If empathy is about living in another person's shoes, great service providers are able to find ways to accommodate the needs of the customer—externally or internally.

2. COMMUNICATION: It's not always about talking. Listening is an especially important tool. Leadership does not have a monopoly on the truth and having clear, open lines of communication allow frontline employees the opportunity to speak truth to leaders. Equally, it's incumbent upon leaders to listen and support corrective actions.

3. CONSISTENCY: Leadership thrives in a consistent environment. The best stewardship creates an environment where partners, employees, and customers have the same expectations. It's the "I know what I am going to get" feeling that you have when you think about a company. Lettuce Entertain You Enterprises is that type of place: where employees and guests have the same equally positive expectations.

CHAPTER 8

UNION SQUARE HOSPITALITY: START AT SQUARE ONE—HIRING

"As I tell people: We are not the most revolutionary company in the world. But I would tell you that we could be the most evolutionary company, because the world has changed and the industry has changed, and we're still thriving. I don't say that with arrogance. I say that with pride." **—RICHARD CORAINE**

IT ALL STARTED WITH UNION SQUARE CAFE

One of my first "real" restaurant jobs was at Union Square Cafe in New York City in 1991, a few years before Richard Coraine—the focus of this chapter—arrived on the scene. The restaurant had been opened by Danny Meyer in 1985. At that time, dining out in New York City (and around the country for that matter) was a pretty formal affair. The magic Meyer brought to the restaurant was that the experience, from the food to the service to the ambiance, was both extraordinarily good and lacking in typical fine-dining formality, replacing a stuffy scene with a sense of warmth and caring.

I worked in the kitchen at Union Square Cafe for three years.

I still remember walking toward the restaurant early one morning and running into Danny Meyer on the street. I had been at the restaurant for only a few months, but he recognized me, and we had a "real" five-minute conversation on the street. To this day, Meyer's genuine effort to engage me that morning planted the seeds for my future career in the hospitality business and beyond. It showed me that he understood the value of nurturing his employees, regardless of their tenure.

When Richard joined Meyer in 1996, Meyer's portfolio consisted of two restaurants, Union Square Cafe and Gramercy Tavern, both up-scale white tablecloth venues. Since then the duo has nurtured Meyer's vision and overseen tremendous growth in the last twenty-two years. Today, the company they have built, Union Square Hospitality Group (USHG), includes eighteen restaurants, a catering and consulting company, as well as an investment arm called Enlightened Hospitality Investments.

Richard, whose official title is chief of staff, describes his business partnership with Meyer as a "Lennon and McCartney thing and whoever is the more talented of those two, I'm the other guy." I think the analogy is spot on, though I would say each is talented in different ways. The synergy between Lennon and McCartney made the Beatles electrifying, but each approached his craft differently and brought a different skill set to the table. The best way I can describe it is that Meyer and Richard collaborate in the same way Lennon and McCartney did on their masterwork "A Day in the Life," ranked number one on *Rolling Stone*'s "100 Greatest Beatles Songs" list. John Lennon wrote the melody and most of the lyrics, but Paul McCartney wrote the middle section and had the idea of adding classical musicians. Both the Beatles and Union Square Hospitality Group demonstrate how two very different people working together can create something revolutionary and excellent.

Richard gives Meyer credit for growing the organization and staying true to its mission, which is based on a philosophy of service that Richard calls "enlightened hospitality" (more on this in a bit). According to Richard, when the two first became partners, Meyer had a lot of revolutionary ideas he wanted to implement, like selling good food at a sports stadium. And, because he "doesn't like to be told what to do," Meyer wasn't asking for advice on how to set up his company; he also didn't care if others thought his ideas wouldn't work. That drive to constantly evolve is what drives the organization to this day.

"When we first got together, [Meyer] had all these crazy ideas which you sort of see in the marketplace now, where he would say, 'Well why couldn't we do food at a bowling alley? That food is never any good. Why couldn't we go to sports stadiums? That food is never any good.' He kept spouting out all these things. He's beyond a good dreamer. He's actually sort of unique in his way to foresee things that would bring people together, right? That's how we create this. We try to become magnets for communities."

YOU CAN'T SPELL CULTURE WITHOUT "CULT"

This idea of being magnets for communities, gathering places where people come together, is at the heart of the USHG philosophy. Although it's a private company, with estimated earnings of up to $500 million, Richard says the goal has never been to attract private equity and go public. Instead, he says, the goal has always been—and will continue to be—to fill gaps in neighborhoods. He cites the USHG venue Daily Provisions, a self-described "neighborhood coffee shop, bakery, and sandwich shop" in New York City, as a typical example: "It was basically created as a place for people to get coffee in the morning and sandwiches and take a roast chicken home at night. We try to add stuff to the community."

This made me curious about how hourly USHG employees would describe their workplaces. Would they speak about community, enlightened hospitality, or something completely different? As we all know, if an organization's culture is not internalized by the line employees, it won't be noticed by their customers.

Richard pauses and leans back before answering.

"You would hear [from employees] derivatives of community and it might come out like family. It might come out like culture, but somebody said to me a while ago, 'You guys are a cult.' I said, 'Thank you,' and they're like, 'Why did you thank me?' I said, 'Well cult is a derivative of culture. You're actually giving me a compliment and saying we're very tight in terms of what the patterns of behavior are.' I look at that as a compliment."

Upon reflection, the idea that USHG is like a cult makes a lot of sense, especially in light of the other organizations that are profiled in the book. People start businesses every day for many reasons, but passionate leaders who believe in a mission, implement a plan to make it happen, and achieve a high level of success are rare. It's why Brooklyn Brewery, Zingerman's, Hyatt, and others remain at the top of their game in extremely competitive industries. Employees at these places really do "drink the Kool-Aid"—and I mean that as a compliment. It is truly flavorful and delicious Kool-Aid.

A key component of USHG's success, Richard says, is the belief in a "cycle of enlightened hospitality": a self-sustaining circle with people at all levels who find joy by bringing it to others, as well as accountability from top to bottom. This is the bedrock of USHG, and the vision that guides every employee. Because there are so many USHG eateries in New York City and some beyond, and because the company is constantly growing, executive leaders cannot be present in each unit on a daily basis. As a result, it's imperative for every employee to internalize the USHG philosophy. Achieving this, Richard says, is all about who you hire, the tools you give them to do the job, and the daily work environment.

"If the people that you hire embody what you want that vision to be, [and] you give them proper training tools and support, and the work environment is one of trust, appreciation, and clarity, you're going to be fairly good at whatever you want to do."

As the self-proclaimed "Lipitor of the company," Richard views his role as eliminating dysfunction in the same way that medicine lowers cholesterol. He said he decided to "go full CSI" on his own company, looking for examples of where the business succeeded and where it failed. What he discovered, he says, was not some profound truth, but the realization that people crave clarity. They want to know what is expected of them and how to avoid mistakes so that they can succeed within the organization. It's the same truth that Nick Sarillo discovered and the reason his pizzerias have such detailed instructions for every job.

To get the point across, Richard goes into full storytelling mode, regaling me with an account of what happened to his friend's uncle when he was in the military.

"One of the first things that happened to his uncle was he became demoralized by his superior who told him to clean the kitchen. His uncle goes in there and he cleans the kitchen. He even had a toothbrush and he did every part of the kitchen. His [supervising officer] came back and said, 'I want to talk to you.' His uncle thought he was going to get a medal but his [supervising officer] said, 'You missed ten things.' He went under a table and said, "How could you miss that?' He went on the floor and said, 'How could you miss that? This kitchen isn't clean. Go clean the kitchen.' The learning in that is if his [supervising officer] had said, 'Here's what a clean kitchen looks like,' he might have been able to not only do that, but also polish it up and then he would have been a hero."

The lesson Richard internalized is that *showing* people what success looks like is much more effective than *telling* them what you want them to do. The second thing he believes is that employees need honest, positive, feedback whenever possible. For this reason, he and other managers expend an enormous amount of energy cheerleading the staff, something many leaders in organizations don't do, he says, because they're so focused on what went wrong, not what went right.

The next idea in his "success toolbox" is something I had never thought of. Though I know it's standard procedure for classroom teachers everywhere, I hadn't considered it in a hospitality context: find out how employees learn best and present the material that way. It's a lesson he took to heart when he was working with two people training to be maître d's, Lauren and Derick. Richard told each of them he'd be showing them their responsibilities and asked how they wanted to get their feedback. It turned out Lauren wanted to get the feedback at the end of the shift so she could ask questions and think about how to get better the next day. Derick, however, wanted to be corrected immediately. Richard asked Lauren why she didn't want to be corrected during the training.

"She told me that would be demoralizing, because if I corrected her, she would be thinking about how bad she was, not the next guest."

Asking the employees how they wanted to learn offered a valuable lesson, he says, because in many situations, managers correct errors on the spot. However, that would have backfired with Lauren, and she would not have succeeded in the job she'd been hired for. By asking how they wanted their feedback, Richard enabled Lauren and Derick to choose the path to success that was right for them.

Offering a level playing field is another essential component to good management, says Richard, and in his mind, it's the final piece of the employee-success puzzle. He also argues that many organizations fail to follow through on their promises to do this, and as a result, it's totally natural that employees would check out if they perceive they are in a game they can never win. People need to know they will rise in an organization based on merit, not connections.

Of course, it doesn't hurt that USHG employees have such a wide range of workplaces and job categories to choose from as long as openings exist, ranging from Union Square Events (private catering) to Shake Shack and The Modern, a high-end restaurant in New York City. This diversity of dining establishment was on purpose, says Richard. It's a way to attract talented people to certain venues and positions and keep them there. This idea of providing diverse opportunities for growth and easy paths for employees to transfer from one unit/concept to another is a mainstay for organizations interested in keeping their best and brightest. It has certainly worked well at USHG.

HIRING EMPATHY

Attracting and retaining talented employees is important to USHG's success, and it all starts with the interview, where USHG leaders try to determine whether a candidate has empathy. Richard says he has only three questions for all potential hires, managers and line employees alike.

"The first one is, 'What is the biggest misperception of you by other people?' *Misperception.* Then refute that for me. You have to do two things. You have to tell me how you think the world sees you and then you have to say, 'I know I send out those messages, but that's not who I really am. Here's who I really am.' You get two answers for one question. The second is 'What's the last gift you gave anybody for any reason?' That shows your ability to give something to somebody else without asking for something in return. Welcome to the restaurant hospitality business. It's what we all do, right?"

At this point, Richard starts beaming as he shares the story of the best answer he ever got to the second question, and it's so good that I'm sharing it too.

"I asked this question and the guy, as soon as I ask it, sits up and gets the biggest smile on his face. Right now, he's ready to tell me about a gift he gave and he's excited and he's smiling. It makes him happy to tell the story. I probably don't even need to continue with this guy, but it gets better."

"'The last gift I gave anybody was I cooked dinner for my girlfriend.'"

"I'm like, 'Okay want to tell me more?'"

"He says, 'Yeah.'"

"Now there's more. Again, here's a guy that's excited to tell you about a gift he gave. Not about him, about what he did for some-body else.

"So he said, 'I cooked her favorite halibut for her birthday.'"

"'Okay. Tell me more.'"

"'Well, I took the day off of work.'"

"That's a sacrifice, right? He's not even going into work to make somebody happy."

"I got the recipe for this halibut and I went down to the fish market at 5 a.m. because somebody told me that's when all the chefs go to buy the best fish. I saw a guy wearing a chef's coat and I said, 'Can you help me find the best halibut?'"

Richard pauses, "Now we've got a guy that has high standards. Only wants the best. Sacrifice, excited to tell me about something he did for somebody else, and has very high standards. He's getting hired."

"'I got the halibut and then I went to the green market and I saw a guy in a white coat too. I said, "Can you help me get the best toma-toes?" They all helped me get the best tomatoes. Then I went home at noon and I made the recipe one time so I could master it before my girlfriend got home.'"

Richard pauses again and makes sure I'm paying attention. I am riveted. This is also the best answer to an interview question I've ever heard. Once he's sure he's got my attention, he continues.

"All this comes from one question. It gets better. Now we've got a guy that doesn't like to fail. He wants it to be good. He doesn't want to ruin somebody's birthday."

"'I made the recipe and it came out. I didn't want to eat it because I wasn't hungry. I took it down to my doorman and I surprised him with lunch. He had never had lunch given to him like that, so I made his day.'"

Another pause. "Didn't even get to his girlfriend yet and he's already got this, right? Then he said, 'My girlfriend came home and I had already cooked it, so I mastered the recipe and I cooked it and she said it was the best surprise she had ever had and it was the best birthday she ever had.'"

I see why that's such a simple yet brilliant question when hiring for a hospitality position. It gets to the heart of putting empathy into action, the core of creating a culture of outstanding service. After all, who would you rather have serving your customers, the guy who gives an Amazon gift card to his girlfriend or the guy who wakes up at 5 a.m. to surprise her with a special dinner? I know who I'd hire hands down.

Finally, he tells me his third interview question, "Who do you admire for any reason?" He uses it because it uncovers another character trait, aspiration. And then, just like before, he launches into a great story about the best answer to that question he ever received. It's so remarkable that I have to share this one too.

"It was a woman. I bet she was nineteen years old. I'll give you the punch line. Ultimately got hired, ran reservations at Eleven Madison Park, maybe the best reservationist we've ever had. Here's the answer to that question, Who do you admire for any reason?"

"'My dad.'"

"I say, 'Okay, why?'"

"'He taught me how to be a good parent. My dad was a single parent, but . . . he had a drug problem and he was in prison. I had to raise my brothers and sisters. I have a brother and a sister younger than me. I had to raise them, but my dad was so committed to the family staying together, he would call me every night from prison and we would talk about my day and what happened with my brother and sister. He tried to give me tips on how I could be a better caretaker. I understand he had legal problems, but he cared so much, that even from jail, he was trying to help me parent. I have a lot of admiration because he could have just stayed there and I would have been on my own. What my skills are, I learned from my dad.'"

Richard looks at me. "That's, 'Who do you admire for any reason?'"

All of those questions reveal something about a person's empathy, so I want to know if Richard thinks measuring empathy is possible. Some of the business leaders I talked to think it's impossible to measure. Even though they know how essential it is in providing quality customer service, they consider trying to measure it an impossible task, like trying to prove the existence of God. Although they deeply believe a high level of empathy separates their employees and the service they provide from their competitors, they say there's no way to quantify it. I ask Richard if he believes empathy can be measured, since he obviously thinks it's an essential attribute for the people he hires.

"There is some truth to the impossibility of measuring it. You know? Because it's done by human beings. We're not robots. We're not programmed, so we're influenced by a lot of different things. There's a lot of logic in not being able to measure it and again, I think what we've found is that you just sort of know it when you see it."

And then he's off telling another great story to illustrate how a truly empathetic hospitality professional acts.

One night he was travelling to give a speech at another company about USHG, and he checked in to his hotel very late. Once he got up to his room, he ordered a bowl of soup, crackers, and water from the woman working the graveyard shift. Richard says she didn't know who he was, but her reaction exemplified empathy.

"She goes, 'Are you feeling okay?'"

"I said, 'Yeah, I'm fine. Why?'"

"She said, 'Well, that's an order I get when people are sick and if you're sick, I'd feel terrible and I'd want to see if there's anything else we could do for you.'"

"I said, 'No, I'm just making a speech. I wanted something light, so I could go to bed.'"

"She's like, 'I feel so much better. Let me get your soup and crackers up to you in the next five minutes so you can go right to sleep. I'm so glad you're not sick.'"

"End of story. I don't know who she is. That had such an impact on me. Here's the three traits that she had that I would say anyone that excels in hospitality has. The easy way to remember is to think about *The Wizard of Oz*. You need a heart, you need a brain, and you need courage. Let's start with the heart. She said, 'Oh, my God, are you okay?' That's an order when people get sick. If you are sick, I'd feel terrible.' Her heart is right there."

"Her brain was, chicken soup plus crackers plus water equals sick. Then her courage was taking the next step because nowhere in the training manual did it say, 'If somebody orders this, ask them if they're sick.'"

"She had enough courage to actually go out there and ask, 'Are you okay?' That's not something that's always trainable. She was wired to do that. I would say that if you look at really great relationship builders and people that are empathetic and caretakers at their core, they have those three things."

HOW USHG OPERATES IN THE DIGITAL AGE

From talking with Richard, it's clear to me that he believes technology can never replace the "heart, brain, and courage" (his words) of genuine human interaction. Nevertheless, we live in a 24/7 digital world. In the past, if customers were really angry, they'd either bring it to the manager's attention at the time or sit down the next day and write a letter. Now they go online and post on Yelp or Snapchat about their experiences. It can be a good way to get feedback if you use it correctly, so I was curious about the digital tools USHG uses to measure quality.

"We look at Yelp," says Richard. "We look at any way that data comes in now digitally and see how that manifests itself or reveals itself [and says something about] the operation. The question is, what do you do with the data? You look to see if it's a pattern. You look to see if it's an isolated thing. Then it's sort of self-correcting because you know where to look. We do quizzes. We do modules of training at every staff meeting. It's a culture of education, which I think it's always been."

He believes new technology has ushered in a better customer experience, which is the primary goal. USHG recently started using Resy, an app that sends texts when tables are ready, and managers use Apple watches to streamline communication, so if someone wants a bottle of wine, the wine steward can be alerted immediately.

"It's not like something buzzes and a robot brings the wine. It's a person that now has sort of a more efficient way to do that. [He] goes and gets the wine and brings it to the customer faster. It's still opened by a human being that's glad to be serving it. It's a tool." Richard's description reminds me a bit of Jerrod Melman's. He also said that technology is a tool to make the customer experience better, but that it's not a substitute for empathy.

LEANING INTO MILLENNIALS

It seems pretty clear to me that the millennial generation is different than the ones that came before it because of how deeply technology is integrated into every aspect of their lives. Research by Espinoza and Ukleja, the authors of *Managing the Millennials*, and Lee Caraher, the author of *Millennials & Management*—and many others—makes a convincing case for this.

"Because of technology, millennials are the first generation that does not need an authority figure to access information," write Espinoza and Ukleja. "Consequently, millennials do not have a felt need to initiate a relationship with authority figures."[15]

That said, some of the subjects of this book, most notably Ari Weinzweig, were offended at the idea that it's possible to assign characteristics to an entire generation. They disagreed that there is any difference between the generations. I wondered what Richard's opinion was. Did he think technology was affecting his younger employees especially? Did he see a difference between the generations?

Richard takes a middle path, noting both similarities and differences between his employees. He believes that everyone, no matter who they are, wants to *matter* as a human being and as an employee in an organization. It's incumbent on the people in charge to get this message across to their diverse workforce.

"The people that are really good figure out how to communicate with all those people so everybody can digest the information in a way that is meaningful to them. You just can't placate the millennials, for example, because you've got a whole workforce here or a whole customer population of which they're just one [part]. I try to be as well-rounded as I can. I watch twenty minutes of MTV a night to get that sort of culture. If there's a song playing, I don't want to be the old

15 Chip Espinoza and Mick Ukleja. *Managing the Millennials: Discover the Core Competencies for Managing Today's Workforce* (Hoboken, NJ: John Wiley & Sons, 2016), 17–18.

guy. Over here, I'm watching *SportsCenter* for fifteen minutes in case somebody wants to talk about the Yankees. I've got to feel that I can maneuver in that way. It's hard."

We then move on and discuss the relationship between accountability and millennials, which is something that everyone else I spoke to for this book feels is critically important. In my early days at Union Square Cafe, the core culture was the same, but the management philosophy leaned toward a more traditional, top-down style, especially in the kitchen where I worked. From my conversations with Richard, it seems clear that the management philosophy has evolved. USHG managers are accountable to their team members because they treat them with respect and act genuinely. There is no resentment about all the care and training lavished upon younger employees, who may not stay for long. The team is focused on meeting each individual employee "where they're at," to use Richard's phrase.

As Richard explains it, "I need to make sure that as long as they're here, they're embodying what we want and I'm fulfilling their desire to matter. I do realize it's got an expiration date. I can't wish that they're going to stay here for twenty-two years like I have. I'm from a different generation. I can't expect everybody to sign up for ten years or twenty-two years here. I've got to get the best of them while they're fully here. People are perishable too. We've got to make sure that we get the best of them for as long as we can."

Like Mike McDerment who was profiled earlier, Richard understands that millennials have myriad choices when it comes to where to shop, what brands to buy, and where to work. To them, loyalty is a two-way street. And as I've already noted, it's not given unless certain criteria—such as authenticity and positive culture—are met.

Speaking about this, Richard notes, "The millennials will not eat the same thing forever like their parents did; [it's] 'Give me a reason not to like Chipotle and I'm gone' as opposed to, 'You can always count on me.' I think that was a big learning [curve] for me. As a result, USHG has to up its game and provide a good reason for these younger employees to stick around as long as they are contributing to the company's goals and values.

The flip side of this issue of millennial loyalty is the high value they place on meaning and authenticity, something we all crave from our interactions. Thus, if you hire empathetic young people, train them well, and treat them well, they're likely to deliver good if not outstanding service. This makes a big difference, because wasting time can be even more irritating than wasting money. This truth is stressed to all employees at USHG, but not at all companies, as we're well aware.

"Nobody has too much time, and I don't want to waste it because I'm never getting it back. If I come here for an hour, make it a good hour for me. I need to leave a little better than when I came in. I gave you something very sacred to me. My time. I think people, operators, businesses take that for granted."

UNION SQUARE HOSPITALITY GROUP'S RECIPE FOR SUCCESS

Union Square Hospitality Group is a model for the restaurant industry. Both Danny Meyer and Richard Coraine have infused their organization with a sense of purpose that stretches from the employees to customers to shareholders—each with a place in the circle of enlightened hospitality. But, as Richard will tell you, their success does not come from fairy dust and unicorns. It comes from consistent hard work and an unwavering belief in the principles that guide daily operations.

1. Encourage curiosity at all levels. At Union Square Hospitality Group, everybody—from the restaurant general manager to the busboy—is encouraged to be part of the hospitality culture. In order to succeed

at that task, you have to be "present" and genuinely engaged with your employees, your customers, and your coworkers.

2. Treat people with respect. While this may seem like an obvious point, Richard Coraine talks about the difference between politeness and empathy—walking in another's shoes. Understanding this difference is the key to creating excellent service. Treating people with respect is a circular, self-fulfilling management tool where respect is both given and received.

3. Offer opportunities for advancement. Your employees are the key to your success. Providing a clearly defined path for advancement helps foster a loyal work environment.

4. Be accountable. Exceptional leaders are accountable to everybody in the organization. It's just that simple.

When I think back to my conversation with Danny Meyer that day outside Union Square Cafe all those years ago, I realize that that interaction embodies so many of the values of any successful service organization. And yet, it was such a simple encounter, one I am sure Danny does not remember. Still, he demonstrated a genuine curiosity about me; he knew who I was and my role in the organization, told me how much he appreciated my effort, and thanked me for being a part of the Union Square team.

In the end, USHG, like all the organizations profiled in this book, demonstrates an absolute commitment to consistent, daily excellence, especially when it comes to executing the company's mission across the breadth of the organization. This can only be achieved if the leadership genuinely believes in the mission. There is no room for half measures; great service providers are "all in" and develop the tools to ensure that outstanding service delivery happens every day.

CHAPTER 9

HYATT:
TOP-DOWN EMPATHY

"The thing I've been reinforcing to people is you cannot practice empathy and be on the clock. You have to take that extra moment. It doesn't take an extra five minutes, but it does take an extra minute. You have to be willing to be there and engage in a way that gets you the nonautomatic responses that you will get. It's hard in a business where efficiency is critical." **—MARK HOPLAMAZIAN**

A HISTORY OF HOSPITALITY

As president and CEO of Hyatt Hotels Corporation, Mark Hoplamazian focuses on instilling the concepts of empathy and action in the company's 110,000 plus employees. This not-so-small army oversees a hospitality empire that spans seven hundred properties, fifty-six countries, and six continents.

Unlike most of the other leaders interviewed in this book, it's impossible for Hoplamazian to interact personally with all the people in his organization. This distance interested me, and I sought him out precisely because I wanted to know how he has promoted the culture of hospitality that Hyatt is known for within such a large and diverse group of people.

I have known Mark for many years, and he has always struck me as an especially thoughtful person, more likely to listen than dictate an opinion. From my perspective, this trait has served him well after he stepped into the role of Hyatt CEO and began to incorporate a new way of thinking at this venerable hotel company.

As you might imagine, Mark is a very busy man, but we finally met in his home in downtown Chicago, where I experienced firsthand his hospitality. He is a naturally gracious host, and upon my arrival I was greeted with wine and cheese. More importantly, when we began our discussion, it was obvious that Mark was engaged. He has well-developed listening skills—something I am sure he has purposefully refined, and which undoubtedly serve him well.

Mark initially became involved with Hyatt in 2006, when he was asked to serve as the interim president of the company. Before ascending to the top job, he was president of the Pritzker Organization, the privately held investment company founded by the Pritzker family and based in Chicago. He had worked in various capacities for Pritzker, one of which was managing the hotel business on the investment side. So, in his words, he'd "been around" Hyatt, absorbing the hospitality culture, in various capacities for seventeen years.

Though he didn't have a traditional hospitality background, he says he always noticed something exceptional about the people at Hyatt.

"I had basically fallen in love with the people. I'd always thought the culture was really cool because there seemed to be such a sense of family and emotional connectivity, and I always thought that was amazing. It felt like people were best friends at work the whole time."

They were, he says, quite a contrast from the people he was used to meeting on Wall Street, and he found the connectivity and engagement in the hotel business intoxicating. Moreover, his "business brain" told him that the hotel company had huge growth potential in large part because of its culture, so he decided to take on the challenge of "setting a direction and taking the company forward" and moved from being an interim president to full-time president and CEO.

He immediately got to work. "The first thing I did was say, 'We need a chief human resources officer.' The company never had one before. I said, 'This is a people business. We really need someone who is going to bring great HR practices.' It was intuitive. Like, 'Of course we need someone who is going to help with culture and leading an effort to bring great practices.'"

HYATT CULTURE IS THE REAL DEAL

When someone with no experience in hospitality intuitively grasps how important hospitality is, my antennae go up. I wanted to know what in Mark's DNA led him to instinctively "know" what eludes so many others, so I asked him to delve into specifics. After pausing and thinking a bit, he spoke about Hyatt's *purpose*. Like all the other leaders in the book, Mark believes every great organization must be able to bring purpose into the workplace.

Remember, Mark had no previous hospitality experience and was starting from scratch. All he really had to rely on was his intuition, honed from his long tenure at Pritzker, and it took him some time to get a true grip on the Hyatt culture. After he'd been running the company for about a year, he began to crystalize his thoughts. As Mark tells it, "I'm interviewing this guy for chief HR officer and he said, 'What is it that's really bothering you right now? What's an issue that's really eating away at you?'"

As he was thinking, the first thing that came to Mark's mind wasn't Hyatt—it was a pharmaceutical company he had helped establish and then sell. "I was involved in something where the product helps to save people's lives. That's a seriously inspirational thing to be able to show up to work for. I said, 'You know? For the life of me, I feel the same way about Hyatt [as I did the pharmaceutical company]. For me, there's something special here, but I can't quite put my finger on it. I'm not sure I know how to characterize it, how to describe it to someone else.'"

At that point, a light bulb went off, and Mark set out to discover exactly what it was in Hyatt's culture that made him feel the same way he did while he worked with the pharmaceutical company, where he felt like he was saving someone's life every day.

"I went back to the management team and I said there's definitely something here that I need to tap into. This is how we ended up going down the path of discussing and describing purpose, what our purpose was as a company and really fundamental questions like 'Why you exist,' not in the conceptual, 'If Hyatt were a color, what color would it be?' kind of bullshit but a very practical one. Ultimately, what we came down to was the sense of care that everyone felt for one another. It's that special cultural, emotional connectivity that caused me to join the company." It seems Mark had figured out what was bothering him.

Once he started asking employees about purpose, he found that they agreed with him. They acknowledged that the reason so many stayed with the company long-term was because of the "emotional connectivity" they had with colleagues.

However, Mark also had a follow-up question. "I would ask people, 'If we went out into the lobby right now and invited a whole bunch of guests to come and join this discussion, and we asked *them* . . . to write down on a piece of paper what they were feeling—what their emotional connection or experience at Hyatt was—would the words look the same?'"

The response was "definitely not." This motivated Mark to go on a mission to find out why. Ultimately, he decided that Hyatt, like many companies, was overrun with procedures. Of course, every company needs processes, but Mark found the desire to "standardize and scrutinize" with formalized scripts wasn't leading to better customer service. Instead it was doing the opposite: putting distance between the guests and staff. This led him to another realization shared by all the leaders in this book: happy employees give better service to customers.

"At that point, my observation was, 'This is killing us. We can't differentiate who we are from a customer service engagement perspective if we're going to try to follow a bunch of rules and suck the humanity out of us. You need to be able to be yourself.'"

With that in mind, Mark and the leadership team set out to help employees feel more at ease. They began with the very basics: uniforms.

"We realized that a lot of people didn't like their uniforms. A lot of the women expressed not feeling like they looked good in them, and they didn't feel self-confident showing up to work. We said, 'Why are we superimposing this from Chicago?'"

They experimented with a hotel in London, allowing the staff to choose the uniforms they wanted. Success! Next came personal grooming.

"A lot of long-time hoteliers were like, 'We can't just let people wear their hair any way that they want. It has to be pulled back in a bun' and 'Here are the rules with respect to tattoos and piercings and you name it.'"

"We really had to get super assertive about saying, 'We're not going to actually set any rules here.' I don't believe that when you take the rules away that people are going to forget about the professionalism that they learned. Frankly, I think it'll take us years to overcome the formalized training. I'm worried about it the other way."

This self-awareness and reflection differentiates Mark from many other leaders I have met over the years. In many ways, his natural inclination to allow others more autonomy is also ideally suited for a management style that rejects top-down philosophy in favor of a flatter management approach. It's not Zappos's holacracy, but it definitely embraces the value of employee involvement in the decision-making process.

"I said, 'They're not going to show up in spiked hair and purple sneakers.' It's not going to happen. Let it go. Some people might need course correction along the way but I'd much rather have that problem than people feeling like they have to follow a bunch of rules when they show up at work. Really, we started down the path of saying, 'We have to change the work conditions in order for people to feel comfortable and be their human selves.'"

His experiment is still a work in progress, especially at Hyatt's premier properties, where some of the leadership teams create what Mark calls a well-intentioned but false narrative about how the guests desire a high level of formality.

"Of course, you don't want to be haphazard and sloppy—you actually have to provide good service. I'm not saying, 'Spill food on people and be thirty minutes late in delivering.' That's not what I'm saying. I'm saying that in the course of your interactions and engagements don't sit there and sweat every single way in which you characterize something. Just be yourself. My expression is 'Authenticity beats perfection every time.' People don't want perfection. They want to know that they're dealing with a real person that cares."

SERVE VS. CARE

As I'm talking with Mark, I'm struck by how quickly he clued into the idea that product quality doesn't necessarily govern how satisfied hotel guests are with their experience. For example, Mark mentions that after he started at Hyatt, he soon realized that although employees in the industry would blame low customer satisfaction scores on outdated hotel designs, he could cite dozens of examples of older hotels receiving top scores.

"Of course, you have to have a good product. You can't sustain great satisfaction over time without a great product, but that's not a key determinant. Any of our competitors could just hire the same designers, build the same thing, same precise room. All you needed was enough money or commitment to do that, so it couldn't be that the product would govern your competitive advantage. It had to be customer service, which was really dependent on the culture of the company."

All of these insights came intuitively to Mark, even though he admits that his lack of experience in the hotel business made him somewhat naive to its challenges. Despite the learning curve, however, being an outsider had some upsides. Sometimes it takes a fresh set of eyes to see things that people working in the trenches for so long may have overlooked, and Mark was motivated to make changes. This was especially true when it came to the company's culture. He strongly believed that Hyatt's culture, which was already good, would respond to expanding the meaning of customer service.

"The big issue there is, what's the difference between 'care' and 'serve'? People within the organization believe that we provide great service, which they pride themselves on. My answer is, 'Great, but serving someone is not caring for them. You can't care for them without serving them, but you can definitely serve them without caring for them.'"

This realization occurred to him when he first became president of the company and began visiting different properties. He said hotel teams went over the top, constantly giving him the best room and amenities even though that wasn't what he asked for. He wanted a standard room so that when people gave feedback he would understand what they were talking about.

He also jokes that he doesn't want to waste time turning off all the lights in a large room. The way he sees it, the GM who didn't want to put him in a standard room thought "the better the room, the better the service" even though it wasn't what Mark wanted or asked for. He recalls throwing a fit at one hotel and forcing the GM to change his room.

"What I got in those early days was the best service, the best room, amazing amenities, but it was a complete and total failure in terms of caring. The practice of empathy is critical. If they really understood why I was asking for the standard room, they would never have given me that suite."

This experience with "room type" embodies the idea of caring vs. service and recalls Mark's opening quote in this chapter. It just takes an extra minute to show the customer that you care. But, the power of that minute has a disproportionate, meaningful effect on the customer's perception of a service interaction.

This breakthrough came to Mark about six months later. "I was meeting with a team in one of the hotels and I said, 'I just want to say thank you for my room because I asked to stay in this particular room type. One of the problems I've had is that nobody before this asked me why, but someone on your team asked me why I wanted to stay in that room. I think that's the key.'"

He then continued with another example, this one involving a well-known entrepreneur who regularly stays in one of Hyatt's hotels. The VIP manager of the hotel kept setting aside a boardroom in the hotel's high-end Regency Club for the man, but he never used it. On his third trip the manager asked him why he was sitting on the couch in the lobby for meetings, not the Regency Club.

The man replied that since he was meeting with entrepreneurs who wanted him to invest in their companies, he needed to get to know them. Sitting around a boardroom table in a formal environment wasn't helpful at all. The entrepreneurs couldn't relax and the industrialist couldn't get a good read on them.

Smiling, Mark skips to the happy ending. "The VIP manager said, 'Well, what I will do is make sure you have a sofa to sit on.' That's the huge difference between service—'Here's this beautiful room'—and care, right? You've got to take that step, practice empathy and then do something about it."

These anecdotes perfectly illustrate my equation: empathy plus action equals hospitality—or "care," to use Mark's vocabulary. That's the key, and the guiding principle that all the leaders in this book strive to transmit to their employees.

PUTTING WORDS INTO ACTION

Visit any tourist city in the world and you'll find a slew of hotels ready to welcome your business. But how do you choose if the price is the same? Mark says he realized early on that customer service was a differentiating factor when it came to this decision—and one that could give Hyatt a competitive advantage. As he sees it, caring—unlike a hotel room—can't be copied. He's a firm believer that customer loyalty is built on the service environment more than the "hardware" of the room.

He says that in order for a culture of caring to permeate every Hyatt property, people have to realize that they're accountable and that leadership takes this value very seriously. If employees can't or won't empathize with guests consistently, they'll be out of a job.

'Ruthless' is too hard of a word, but you've got to be serious about your commitment to this. We've actually let a fair number of GMs go, not just leadership people, but GMs and some people in the corporate office, including people at the top of the organization," says Mark. "It's hard. You sit down with someone and say, 'You've got to go because you're not really abiding by the purpose we've set and our values.' People look at you like, 'You've got to be kidding, right? Have you looked at my numbers? What's the problem?'"

In the end, Mark makes the point that a genuine leader has to be consistent. He says, "The answer is, you've got to make it real . . . because people are not stupid. They see who gets promoted or who is still on board and if people are behaving a certain way and it looks like we condone that, then your credibility is right out the window."

Mark's comments echo something a lawyer told me during a moment in my own business when I needed to fire two key employees because they were not adhering to the company's values. My attorney told me: "The cemetery is full of indispensable people." In the moment, it was tough for me to accept that the long-term benefit of acting in a manner consistent with our overall company values was more important than the pain of losing a top performer. But in the end, my management team was strengthened, and I came to appreciate the value of consistency.

Emphasizing customer service is one way to meet the challenge of running a hotel, and increasing the number of days repeat guests stay in a Hyatt annually is a great way to measure success. Mark gets at this with the perfect analogy. Let's say you love your iPhone, but you only get to use it three or four days a year. Would you be as passionate about it? Probably not. That's the problem with episodic visits. As a result, Hyatt is keenly tracking repeat visits and measuring improvements in year over year performance among individual hotels and brands.

At the end of the day, Mark recognizes the difference between a product (hotel room) and a service (hospitality), and how differentiating them is a tool his organization can use to build stronger loyalty. "Someone could say. 'Mark, God bless you. You're trying to do good work, but it's just not worth it because given travel patterns,

I'm not sure I can get there.' I can understand how people would feel that way," he says. "But from my perspective, you're now relegated to a commoditized approach to business and then product or price are what you try to compete on. And, I think those are short-lived, and they're transactionally based and they're not emotional. You can build a very good hotel company that way, probably do that as long as you continue to scale at spectacular pace, but you'll never build a brand people are passionate about. Those are the brands that end up being the most valuable—the ones that people really care about."

HIRING AND ONBOARDING—LESS IS MORE

In order to put their money where their mouth is, Hyatt has changed how it hires people. The first way they did this was to take their existing employee profile, which had twenty-two competencies, and decrease that to five: care, serve, learn, adapt, and achieve. "Care"—how a person engages with people—is the number one attribute on the list.

Because of this new framework, Mark says it's common now to hire people with no prior hospitality experience. As a professor at DePaul's School of Hospitality Leadership, I wanted to understand why Hyatt made this decision, how they found these new hires, and what characteristics they were looking for in the potential hires. To illustrate the answer, Mark offered yet another anecdote. He told me about how one of Hyatt's boutique hotels in Delhi interviewed job candidates in an offsite bar.

"It was like walking into a party as opposed to an interview room. Several of the people said they were completely confused and wondered if they were really supposed to be there for a job."

Yes, they were. From that group, the managers hired for attitude, not experience, and they wound up with people from food, fashion, and retail backgrounds, all with the personality they wanted. The result?

The leadership team felt confident they had just hired an extremely strong team.

Once people are hired, of course, they need to be onboarded. This is a completely different challenge than hiring and can be tricky when you're dealing with multiple languages and cultures, as Hyatt, a global company, is. As a result, Hyatt has worked with the Stanford University instructional design school (known as the d.school) to help people practice empathy and then translate that into day-to-day operations. This became particularly important to Mark after hearing about one employee's experience working at a hotel that Hyatt had acquired in Mexico.

"It was about a year after we bought it and one of the things we had to do as part of our design thinking training was go and talk to colleagues in the hotel about how we could do a better job of acknowledging people, to recognize people for a job well done. I sat down with the assistant front office manager along with one of our GMs from Latin America."

"I'm interviewing our colleague, and, of course, I'm the CEO and she's terrified. She's like a deer in the headlights. The response to every question I ask her is, 'It's great.' Completely automatic. I'm trying to get her to be in the moment, so I said, 'Why don't you tell me how things have changed since we took over the hotel?'"

"'It's been great.'"

"I said, 'Why don't you tell me about what was it like when we first showed up? Tell me about your first day coming to work when it became a Hyatt. What was that experience like?'"

"'It was great.'"

"I said, 'No. That morning, what time did you get up? Was it sunny outside? How did you get to work?'"

"It took me ten minutes of this to get her into the moment. About five minutes after that, she was in tears. The reason was because she described to me that she had heard all these great things about the Hyatt family and yet her experience over her first two days was to learn all about how she could get fired. It was like chapter and verse on ethics, on foreign corruption practices, on business conduct. I mean, you name it, we had a form for her to sign and all the requirements that we had and all of the violations and what the consequences were."

"She said, 'I'm walking into work. The general manager, the front office manager, and the head of sales, each of whom I liked and learned a lot from, were all gone, replaced with Hyatt people. Now I'm sitting down learning my first two days how I can get fired. Welcome to the Hyatt family.'"

"It blew me away," says Mark. "I was in tears. The GM that was with us was in tears. We walked out of that room with a big lesson."

Mark knew why those forms existed. Legal and HR wanted new employees to comply with company policies in writing and needed signed forms in personnel files as soon as an employee was hired. But they didn't think about things from the new employees' point of view—just their own. Mark knew something had to change.

"What we should have been doing was putting ourselves in the shoes of the person for whom we were designing that process, the new employee. What do you want their experience to be? If you promote the Hyatt family and what our culture is all about and then you show up and you're like the police sitting there raking people across the coals, it's a complete cognitive dissonance. As an emotional matter, it was horrible. And why? Because we didn't put ourselves in the shoes of the person for whom we were designing the process."

The result was a completely revamped onboarding process with lots of room for individual hotels to express how happy they are to have the new employee join the team. One that Mark is particularly proud of is a hotel in Rio de Janeiro. One of the interview questions there is "What person had a significant impact on your life and why?" If the person is hired, HR contacts the new employee's family to get a picture of the person he or she mentioned and tapes it in their work locker so it's there the first day. Now, other hotels within the Hyatt family are copying this idea, and slowly but surely it's spreading throughout the organization.

MARK ON MILLENNIALS

Not surprisingly, Hyatt faces the same challenges as any company when hiring younger, less experienced people. And Hyatt has a lot of young applicants because a hotel is a great place for entry-level employees to look for work. As you know by this point, when it comes to millennials, there are two camps in this book. One believes the new generation of workers is the same as previous generations, and the other notices and then embraces the differences. Mark is in the latter camp. He likes the fact that the younger people he meets want to have a purpose at work and care about what they're doing before they commit to a job.

"A lot of young people, I'm told . . . make their decision in the first ten minutes of the first day. They ask themselves, 'Does this feel right?' It's based on how they feel about it, not about the content, but about the sentiment. They want to care about what they're doing. Like, when they show up to work, is it something they feel is worthy of their time and effort?"

Many books about managing workers today note the supposed differences in attitude between baby boomers and millennials. It's what Mark sees too; in fact, listening to his experience reminds me of many of the anecdotes I read as I researched this topic.

"I just see trade-offs that younger people are prepared to make. Like, 'I'm not really going to commit myself to work those extra three hours this week or today because I really want to maintain life balance and I want to make sure I spend time with my friends.' That thought never crossed my mind. Maybe that's me personally, but in my generation I felt like most of the people I knew were so committed to their career paths and jobs that they worked really, really hard to the exclusion of other things, whereas I see people actually willing to stand up for that life balance stuff, at a much earlier age than I remember experiencing myself, and I see it pretty pervasively."

This idea, that younger people are looking for meaning and community in work in the same way that previous generations found it in their personal, more private lives, such as in places of worship, is something Mike McDerment of FreshBooks mentioned, and I ask Mark if he agrees. He hesitates, thinking before nodding, and then telling me about a meeting he recently attended in Boston with other CEOs and heads of HR from other large corporations like Facebook, Apple, and IBM.

The meeting was dedicated to the question of how to bring a better sense of well-being into the workforce. According to Mark, forward-thinking companies realize that because people are spending so much time at work, employers need to help them become more balanced and promote good mental health, not just physical health.

"People are much more attuned and sensitive to the fact that they do spend a lot more time at work than at home. If you can't be balanced while you're at work, you can't be balanced in life. I thought that was really interesting. The level of focus on this is really, really high. I don't think that's generational. I think that's just a recognition that that's a better way to be."

THE ACCOUNTABILITY BUS IS LEAVING
THE STATION WITH OR WITHOUT US

One of the biggest challenges in a large organization like Hyatt is holding people in leadership positions accountable, no matter where they are in the world. It's something Mark thinks about a lot because he believes that if you make entry-level employees accountable, leadership has to demonstrate accountability too. To illustrate this, he tells me about an experience with his oldest daughter.

"She'll sit me down and say, 'Dad, look. You can't talk to Leo [Mark's youngest son] that way. He doesn't hear you when you do that. This is his experience with you.' She'll explain it to me. I'll be so completely leveled and humble. She's just being plain about it. She's not mean-spirited about it. She's not inappropriate about it. She really is coaching me. That's incredible. I would never have dreamed of doing that."

I give him my perspective: that all the access to and availability of information along with expectations and a need for accountability have reframed the way people, from our children's ages (late teens and early twenties) to those into their early thirties, look at the world. "We can either get on the bus with them or the bus is going to leave without us," I tell him. As is usual with Mark, he listens to me quietly and nods his head in agreement.

Both Mark and I believe that companies that are able to structure themselves around values like accountability and empathy will attract the best and the brightest and those that don't will be left at the station.

HYATT'S RECIPE FOR SUCCESS

In my view, it's pretty clear that the world of Hyatt is creating a new path to exceptional customer service delivery. Not surprisingly, the company's success is a complex recipe but one that does embrace a few consistent, key elements.

1. Care is a scarce but critical commodity. If a sense of care (or empathy) is a core principle in your organization, it's not an unthinkable leap

to nudge the behavior of employees in that direction. As Mark says, "It's not five minutes, but it does take a minute." Practicing empathy can yield disproportionately positive results for that one-minute investment.

2. Be accountable. This theme is neither new nor hard to wrap your mind around but is so easily dismissed in lieu of expediency. However satisfying it might sound, "Because I said so" is not an acceptable rationale for decision-making in today's workplace. Perhaps it was never a good policy, but the top-down management structure will fall on deaf ears among millennials, the majority of today's workforce. Leaders at any level need to make sure their behavior models the expectations of employees and, in the case of Hyatt, it means caring from top to bottom.

3. Hire for fit not for competency. In a large organization—actually, any organization—it's a little scary to prioritize humanity and culture over core competencies and experience. Nonetheless, as long as leaders are clear about expectations and goals, the right attitude will supercede whether the server removes the plate from the right or left side of a guest after they finish their entree. At Hyatt, strong training support has allowed the organization to shift priorities and hire for a new set of values.

Shifting culture in a large organization is like changing the direction of a giant cruise ship. It's definitely a challenge and, undoubtedly, the organization will encounter icebergs. But consistent leadership certainly goes a long way toward navigating a safe passage. I, for one, look forward to observing the voyage. After sitting with Mark, I can't wait to visit more of his hotels to see his ideas for myself!

CHAPTER 10

LESSONS LEARNED

When I was running my own company, I don't think I would have appreciated some of the ideas suggested by the business leaders in this book. The challenges of day-to-day operations made it easy for me to isolate myself into the rigors of operations. After all, I was running multiple restaurants and trying to build a wine brand with all the challenges that you might imagine—from inconsistent product quality to employees drinking on the job. My comfort zone was being "in the weeds" with my team, and it was much easier to bury myself in the crisis of the moment than to step back and try to create a stronger organization for the long run. I didn't invest enough energy in creating the right environment because I didn't appreciate the value of the investment. My success happened in spite of—not because of—my actions.

My first real restaurant job was in London, at Kensington Place. The head chef, Rowley Leigh, led the kitchen with all the discipline and skill you would expect in a classic European environment. Don't get me wrong; he was an exceptional chef and an even more exceptional person, but the kitchen was highly structured. Whatever Chef said was law, and his chef de cuisine followed his lead. In fact, the kitchen was so structured that the schedule was color-coded by job with names listed in order of seniority. There was no question about where you stood in the pecking order.

Thirty years later, I still remember my first week. Chef told the butcher to go help his wife, whose car had broken down at his house. Next thing I knew, the butcher had his coat on and was walking out the door. It was an intimidating environment, and I was scared to come to work every day. It was organized in classic top-down management style—the organizational style that contradicts everything this book and the leaders in it espouse. But, I have to admit, I learned more in that kitchen about food preparation, line cooking, and discipline than any other work experience in my career.

After my stint in London, I ended up at Union Square Cafe in 1992. It was the early days—even before Richard Coraine was on the scene—and I was exposed to a completely different approach to what a restaurant, or any business for that matter, could be. The sense of community and culture were clearly present in those days, and they opened my eyes to an environment that was different. I don't think the USHG vision was as clearly formed at that time as it is today, but the seeds were there.

I tried to incorporate the values of Union Square Cafe in my own business life; yes, I stole a few ideas and took them back to Chicago as I began opening and operating restaurants. But, to be honest, they never really stuck. While the employees were loyal to me and the brand, we never built the kind of long-lasting culture that stood the test of time. Through all the ups and downs of my own career, however, I have increasingly come to understand the important lessons of hospitality, and I wonder how focusing on them might have strengthened my own businesses.

When I introduced the idea of empathy + action early in this book, I mentioned that it's a well-established formula that has been embraced by restaurateurs and others in the industry since the days of the first taverns. But it is still far underused. I have worked for some of the industry's icons and known many others, and I have seen how the lessons of hospitality are often overlooked. I've also learned that there is no roadmap for building a great hospitality organization.

With this book, I have attempted to provide a sort of road map—various recipes for hospitality success, if you will. I have come to appreciate that hospitality, in all its manifestations, is a tool that can be applied across the service economy, whether you operate a local hardware store, a large hospital, a chain of sporting goods stores, or something else. The key to success is to fully embrace many—if not all—of the tenets expressed by the leaders in this book.

So, what are these leaders' lessons for us? Unsurprisingly, everything revolves around values. As I have articulated throughout this book, I think their essential message breaks down into five core values that are each important in their own right, but much more powerful when combined: accountability, authenticity, culture, community, and vision.

ACCOUNTABILITY

The leaders in this book are accountable to themselves and their employees. This manifests itself in a variety of ways. Take Nick Sarillo, for example, of Nick's Pizza & Pub. He has developed a business where not only is he accountable to employees, but they are accountable to one another. He has eliminated the need for any type of job evaluation because performance review is baked into the experiences of Nick's employees' from day one. Despite the fact that he only has three local operations, Nick has taken the time, expense, and brain space to develop a detailed game plan for each member of his team. It's these details that make the Nick's engine run so smoothly and ensure that its pizzas are produced quickly and consistently. His staff is engaged with its guests because each member knows how important quality service is to the bottom line. There are no secrets at Nick's, and that is just the way he likes it.

At the end of the day, what does accountability really mean in the modern workplace? I suspect most leaders believe they are accountable—I certainly thought I was accountable when I ran my business for twenty years. But accountability as defined in this book is more than simply taking abstract responsibility for the actions and the direction of an organization.

True accountability requires selflessness and a willingness to leave your ego at the door. Leaders who are accountable accept the reality that they do not have all the answers. Rather than dictate policy, they create a culture where it's not only safe but equally valued to be a part of the discussion. This is a long way from my London kitchen. Back then, if Chef told me to jump, the only question I asked was how high.

Today, that kind of approach is much less likely to yield long term results—even though it might be efficient in the short-term. As I reflect back on my work history in London, I am reminded that the line employees were never comfortable expressing ideas or concerns. To the contrary, we often just put our collective heads down and tried to stay out of trouble. Even though the kitchen was an amazing, almost magical place in many ways, it could have been even better if employees had felt welcome to contribute their ideas too. Rowley Leigh's extraordinary talent was limited because the structure of the kitchen created an inauthentic environment—the exact opposite of a collaboration. I often wonder how much more fulfilling the experience would have been had circumstances been different—both for myself and the guests of the restaurant. Who knows how much more successful the restaurant could have been?

AUTHENTICITY

Coupled with accountability, authenticity builds the kind of bridge that yields loyalty—from employees and to your brand. Consider Jerrod Melman from Lettuce Entertain You Enterprises. Jerrod is young—a near-millennial in his own right—and he inherently understands the importance of authenticity. In his position—helping manage the largest independent restaurant company in the country, built from the ground up by his father—it would have been easy to simply check boxes and keep the ball rolling. But Jerrod and his siblings have embraced their father's deep passion and genuine love of the restaurant business. As a result, people like Jerrod, who lead by example, are a model for the seventy-five hundred employees who are steeped in the company's culture. There's a good reason that the values of great food, great service, and genuine hospitality are part of the Lettuce experience within its venues across the country. Jerrod Melman isn't pretending. He loves his work, and, like his father, his passion bleeds into every decision and employee, and, ultimately, into the guest experience.

Zappos offers another textbook example of authenticity. As Rob Siefker explained, the Zappos culture, with employee-created murals on the walls and self-decorated work stations throughout the building, is a living and breathing example of how words translate into authentic action. If the workplace didn't represent the philosophy of the company's leadership, it would be apparent when walking the halls of the Las Vegas office. Instead, visitors see physical manifestations of all the values Rob champions.

In my experience, well-intentioned people prefer authenticity over bullshit. It seems like a pretty obvious concept, but think about how many times you encounter an inauthentic customer service experience. One of my favorites is when I am leaving a restaurant and the host, barely looking up, shouts, "Have a good day. Thanks for coming." It's so formulaic and uninspiring that the effort generates a negative feeling in me. Great restaurants, on the other hand, make you feel so good about your visit, like when the host makes eye contact and genuinely asks, "How was your dinner?" or says, "Thank you so much for spending your evening with us." The time and effort is virtually the same, yet the resulting guest experience is completely different. Given that we know that all customers, not just millennials, are looking for meaning and authenticity, it's hard to minimize the importance and value of being in the moment with your customer.

CULTURE

When I first met with Mike McDerment, we took a tour of the FreshBooks headquarters and then had a long discussion about the evolution of his company. And then he started to get a little philosophical. I asked a question about how he could know whether his investments in corporate culture yielded better customer service and whether it was really worth the expense and constant effort. He sat back and responded that it was the FreshBooks culture that gave meaning and a sense of belonging to him and his employees. He said it drove the entire team to be passionate about the company and what it stood for, and, ultimately, fueled better performance internally and externally. Moreover, he was proud and excited that the organizational culture had evolved organically from his own experience and needs. In fact, he went so far as to postulate that the meaning his employees found in their work was akin to religion—providing a grounded place for creativity, community, and passion. The expressions of commitment may not be the same, but the sense of belonging certainly is.

I've read about the merits of developing a strong corporate culture, about sports teams that have "a good locker room," and have heard stories from friends about how their company is a great place to work. Until I met the leaders in this book, however, "culture" remained an elusive term to me. Of course, it *sounds* important—but how does it manifest itself? My interviews changed my beliefs about culture. I now understand that culture is not something to be casually folded into a corporate mission statement. Instead, it's a word that speaks to the identity of an organization and the ways it is unique. A strong, positive culture is a differentiating factor and, if genuine, creates opportunities for employees to grow and then pass on their feelings of belonging to the customers, who buy the products or services. Thus, a thoughtful, productive culture can have far-reaching benefits for a company's bottom line.

However, a strong culture does not arrive fully formed overnight, and it cannot be manufactured like a product; it is a service in and of itself. It certainly cannot be inventoried and, if not nurtured, it will disappear. The leaders in this book have figured out that promoting a particular culture is just as or more—important than anything else they do every day. In fact, I would argue that putting time, thought, and care into developing an extraordinary culture outweighs the benefits of any customer service training or product upgrade. It's easy to talk about it; I know I did when I was an operator. However, like many goals in life, commitment to establishing and maintaining a great company culture is ineffective without concrete actions to develop and support it.

COMMUNITY

Consider Steve Hindy of Brooklyn Brewery. He built a craft beer brand over thirty years ago from the ground up. In that time, no matter what challenges the company faced, he never strayed from his core values. When Steve thinks about community, the concept spreads out from the Brewery to the Brooklyn neighborhood where it all started. He understood that nurturing the community would ultimately nurture his brand. Steve could have tried to take a more expeditious path toward growing the Brewery, but he chose to "keep it real," and, as a result, the Brooklyn Brewery community was born.

Imagine if the sales force hadn't bought into this new craft beer idea in those early days. Do you think the brand would have survived and flourished without the passion Steve demonstrated from day one? And, even today, while the distribution and volume has exploded, Steve continues to hold true to the same principals. He also continues to engage with employees, host events that speak to the Brooklyn Brewery culture, and act as the brand's ambassador in the community. Given the Brewery's success, he could have chosen to step back from those efforts, but building community is in his DNA. The Brewery's employees, Brooklyn, and any place where the beer is sold are the beneficiaries.

I know all of this is true because I have experienced it myself. As an adjunct professor at DePaul University, I have come to appreciate the teaching community within the school as well as its place within the city. I feel part of something bigger than my own department and carry my affiliation as a badge of honor—and I work hard at my job largely because of it. My emotional connection comes from the school's values and the commitment of the dean and my colleagues. Community synthesizes the core values of an organization and manifests itself in the way employees talk about the place they work, the standing of the organization among local residents, and, ultimately, the value both employees and customers receive due to their loyalty to the community.

VISION

Perhaps there is no effort more important than understanding and articulating a clear vision for your company. I think about

Paul Spiegelman of BerylHealth. Paul attributes much of his success in developing a vision for his company to his upbringing. This idea echoes the argument that Susan Salgado, the hospitality consultant, mentioned to me, which is that some people simply have hospitality in their DNA. For Paul, it was instilled by his parents, and he developed a company around the sense of care that they taught him. This interest in caring became the thing that differentiated BerylHealth from its competitors even though the services the company provided were more expensive.

Paul has stuck to his vision and built his mission and values around a core purpose. He chose to hire employees based on a shared set of values, not job skills. He embraced the opportunity to plot a course for his company beyond daily tasks, empowered his managers and employees to own the decision-making process, and by doing so created a collaborative organization. None of the results, personal or financial, would have been realized had Paul not outlined a clear vision for his employees and then created the tools for them to execute it.

I saw how that same emphasis on vision manifests itself at Zingerman's when I ate breakfast with Ari Weinzweig in Ann Arbor. Zingerman's began with a big idea and now embodies it every day through its mission and guiding principles. Adhering to a vision is part of everything—even performance reviews, when managers ask employees to envision where they'll be in a year. This painstaking adherence to an overriding vision has permeated Zingerman's culture and led to an outstanding level of customer service that is recognized far outside Ann Arbor. (And has also led to very healthy earnings.)

Again, I find myself thinking about the difference between words and actions. Corporate mission and vision are part of almost any company's makeup—whether explicit in a larger organization or implicit in a corner hardware store. But, as we have seen over and over again through the examples in this book, what *really* matters is not how the vision sounds, but how it drives community, culture, authenticity, and accountability in a way that really differentiates one company from another. We all look for meaning in life, regardless of how we define it. For some of us, meaning might be spiritual. For others, meaning might come in the form of our relationships to friends and family. It can also come from our workplaces. Any organization that can provide a clear and meaningful vision and reinforce it consistently with concrete actions can truly transform the workplace experience for anyone who is a part of it.

IN THE END . . .

In many ways, the conclusions of each conversation I had circled back to the equation of hospitality spelled out at the beginning of the book. When I reflect on my conversation with Mark Hoplamazian of Hyatt Hotels, his idea about actively demonstrating care encapsulates a genuine understanding of human nature and what it means to create a meaningful workplace experience. Aren't we all hoping for meaning in our work—that is, actual meaning, not just a sweet cliché uttered by top performers? It seems clear to me that incorporating hospitality, true hospitality, throughout an organization is one of the best tools to make employees and customers more satisfied. This satisfaction leads to loyalty across the board, and, ultimately, to increased profitability. It may not be obviously measured by a line item on a balance sheet but metrics like employee attrition and its cost can be tracked—just ask Paul Spiegelman.

Whether they define hospitality in the precise terms I did or not, all the corporate leaders in this book use empathy plus action to create a unique work environment that challenges their employees to be their best selves. Each leader has recognized that a traditional top-down management structure that forces employees into specific tasks, without providing a sense of the bigger cause, is increasingly less compatible with the modern workplace. That's not to imply direction and structure are unimportant for managers and line employees. It would be a mistake to dismiss *all* of the fundamental aspects of organizational development.

Nonetheless, the modern workplace can and should be more meaningful to employees. And if your organization is not, the next generation, the millennials, will find a place that is. As we continue to leap into our increasingly interconnected world, there is an opportunity to create a better workplace environment. It's clear that millennials are looking for a new way forward. While that path is being forged the transition may not always be smooth, but the end results are certainly worth it for employees, customers, and the company's bottom line. As we have seen, it comes down to making a commitment to principles and then sticking to them. In the coming years, as the millennial population continues to increase its purchasing power (and leadership ranks), they will reward companies that align with their personal philosophy. There's no doubt in my mind that this new generation of consumers, and the ones that follow, will still reward a great service experience with loyalty.

I've mentioned how, in retrospect, I might have run my business differently. One of the great benefits of writing a book like this is that you get to revisit past practices and reflect on how they could have been better. It's not easy to recognize one's own shortcomings and appreciate the mistakes for what they are. But, learning from past practice—whether in business or in life—can drive a good leader to be a better one. It's not a cliché to acknowledge that the world is changing quickly. I wish I had been a bit wiser as a leader, but I have learned extraordinary lessons from the people featured in this book.

We can all benefit from learning about the experiences of others. In the end, it's my hope that the stories told in these pages will inspire you to incorporate hospitality in new and unique ways throughout your organization. After all, we put a lot of effort into our work. Why not create experiences for those who work with us that are more engaging, more meaningful, and more inspiring? The result will be a more rewarding life for all of us.

BIBLIOGRAPHY

ADKINS, AMY. "Millennials: The Job-Hopping Generation."
Gallup.com. May 12, 2016. https://www.gallup.com/
businessjournal/191459/millennials-job-hopping-generation.aspx.

BURLINGHAM, BO. *Small Giants: Companies that Choose to be Great Instead
of Big*. New York, NY: Portfolio/Penguin, 2005.

CARAHER, LEE. *Millennials & Management: The Essential Guide to Making It
Work at Work*. Brookline, MA. Dibllomotion, Inc., 2015.

CLIFFORD, CATHERINE. "How One Company Keeps Millennial Employees
from Quitting." CNBC.com. September 19, 2016.
https://www.cnbc.com/2016/09/19/how-one-company-keeps-millennial-
employees-from-quitting.html.

ESPINOZA, CHIP, AND MICK UKLEJA. *Managing the Millennials: Discover
the Core Competencies for Managing Today's Workforce*. Hoboken, NJ:
John Wiley & Sons, 2010.

GREENLEAF, ROBERT K. *Servant Leadership: A Journey into the Nature of
Legitimate Power & Greatness*. Mahwah, NJ: Paulist Press, 1977.

KADAKIA, CRYSTAL. *The Millennial Myth: Transforming Misunderstanding
into Workplace Breakthroughs*. Oakland, CA: Berrett-Koehler Publishers,
Inc., 2017.

KAUFMAN, MICHA. "Five Reasons Half of You Will Be Freelancers in 2020." Forbes.com. February 28, 2014. https://www.forbes.com/sites/michakaufman/2014/02/28/five-reasons-half-of-you-will-be-freelancers-in-2020/#5c86e7696d39.

REICHHELD, FRED. *The Ultimate Question: Driving Good Profits and True Growth*. Boston, MA: Harvard Business School Press, 2006.

REINGOLD, JENNIFER. "How a Radical Shift Left Zappos Reeling." Fortune.com. March 4, 2016. https://fortune.com/zappos-tony-hsieh-holacracy/.

STACK, JACK, AND BO BURLINGHAM. *A Stake in the Outcome: Building a Culture of Ownership for the Long-Term Success of your Business*. New York, NY: Doubleday, 2003.

STACK, JACK, AND BO BURLINGHAM. *The Great Game of Business: The Only Sensible Way to Run a Company*. New York, NY: Random House, 2013.

WEINZWEIG, ARI. *A Lapsed Anarchist's Approach to the Power of Beliefs in Business*. Ann Arbor, MI: Zingerman's Press, 2016.

WEINZWEIG, ARI. *Zingerman's Guide to Giving Great Service*. New York, NY: Hyperion, 2004.

ZEITHAML, VALARIE, BERRY, LEONARD, PARASURAMAN, A. "Communication and Control Processes in the Delivery of Service Quality." *Journal of Marketing,* Vol. 52, Issue 2, 35-48. /1988.

ACKNOWLEDGMENTS

We would like to thank our parents, Martie and Bob, who always told us we'd get along one day, even when we weren't so sure. Thank you for your love and support.

To Bo Burlingham, who was so generous with his time and connections.

Thank you to all the leaders featured in this book along with their team members, assistants, and coworkers who patiently answered questions and freely gave their time and insight.

Thanks to Alex Merrill, publisher at Apollo and good friend. Your kind and persistent enthusiasm for this project turned it from a conversation over a beer into a manuscript. And, thanks to Julia Abramoff and Adam Rosen for all their support, constructive criticism, and sound advice along the way.

JANET SPECIFIC

I would like to express my deep and sincere gratitude to everyone who encouraged me throughout this project. You know who you are!

I also want to thank my husband, Emmon, for his enthusiastic support, advice, and eternal optimism. Special shout-outs to my children, Cameron and Miranda, and to Sara Tipton for her constructive suggestions.

Last but certainly not least, I would also like to thank my brother, Dan, who helped me fulfill a lifelong dream of writing a book.

DAN SPECIFIC

Thank you, Naomi, who has encouraged me to pursue my interests and passions. Your input has been invaluable even when I don't want to admit it. I am so lucky to spend days and nights with you. Thanks Madeline, Nina, and Benjamin . . . you inspire me every day.

The truth is that this book NEVER would had been written without the patience, dedication, and intelligence of my sister, Janet. You were the best cowriter I could have asked for and made this "work" easy.